# Coaching for Schools

# About the author

Judith Tolhurst is a highly respected coach in the field of education. She currently runs a successful coaching practice working with school leaders and also trains school leaders and staff in coaching skills. She has over twenty five years of experience within education having held many leadership roles in a variety of settings including headship.

She is committed to developing the potential of staff in schools and believes wholeheartedly in enabling schools to build their own leadership capacity. She currently delivers a range of progammes for the National College for School Leadership as well as her own courses. She currently works with school leaders coaching them around leadership issues and providing support.

Judith runs a company called Coachlamp which is committed to bringing coaching skills and practices to schools. She can be contacted by e-mail: judith.tolhurst@coachingforschools.co.uk or via the web: www.coachingforschools.co.uk.

# Coaching for Schools

A practical guide to
building leadership capacity

Judith Tolhurst

Harlow, England • London • New York • Boston • San Francisco • Toronto
Sydney • Tokyo • Singapore • Hong Kong • Seoul • Taipei • New Delhi
Cape Town • Madrid • Mexico City • Amsterdam • Munich • Paris • Milan

PEARSON EDUCATION LIMITED

Edinburgh Gate
Harlow CM20 2JE
Tel: +44 (0) 1279 623623
Fax: +44 (0) 1279 431059
Website: www.pearsoned.co.uk

First published in Great Britain in 2006

© Pearson Education Limited 2006

The right of Judith Tolhurst to be identified as author of this work has been asserted by her in accordance with the Copyright, Designs and Patents Act 1988.

ISBN-13: 978-1-4058-2196-4

British Library Cataloguing-in-Publication Data
A catalogue record for this book is available from the British Library

Library of Congress Cataloging-in-Publication Data

Tolhurst, Judith.
    Coaching for schools : a practical guide to building leadership capacity / Judith Tolhurst.
      p. cm.
    Includes index.
    ISBN-13: 978-1-4058-2196-4
    ISBN-10: 1-4058-2196-5
    1. Mentoring in education.  I. Title.
  LB1731.4.T65 2006
  371.102—dc22

2006048332

All rights reserved. No part of this publication may be reproduced, stored in a retrieval system, or transmitted in any form or by any means, electronic, mechanical, photocopying, recording or otherwise, without either the prior written permission of the Publisher or a licence permitting restricted copying in the United Kingdom issued by the Copyright Licensing Agency Ltd, Saffron House, 6–10 Kirby Street, London EC1N 8TS. This book may not be lent, resold, hired out or otherwise disposed of by way of trade in any form of binding or cover other than that in which it is published, without the prior consent of the Publishers.

10 9 8 7 6 5 4 3 2
10 09 08 07

Typeset in 11.25/14pt Minion by 35
Printed and bound in Great Britain by Henry Ling Limited, at the Dorset Press, Dorchester, DT1 1HD

*The Publisher's policy is to use paper manufactured from sustainable forests.*

# Table of contents

|  |  |  |
|---|---|---|
|  | Publisher's acknowledgements | vi |
|  | Author's acknowledgements | vii |
|  | Preface | viii |
| Chapter One | What is coaching? | 1 |
| Chapter Two | The essential skills of coaching | 24 |
| Chapter Three | The coaching process | 53 |
| Chapter Four | How to develop a coaching culture in your school | 81 |
| Chapter Five | Coaching to make a difference | 102 |
| Chapter Six | Coaching and performance management | 120 |
| Chapter Seven | Coaching and middle leadership | 146 |
| Chapter Eight | Coaching and strategic development | 173 |
| Chapter Nine | Coaching the team | 194 |
| Chapter Ten | Coaching and distributed leadership | 219 |
|  | Index | 246 |

# Publisher's acknowledgements

We are grateful to the following for permission to reproduce copyright material:

Figure 8.2 from Adair, J., *The Concise Adair on Team Building and Motiviation*, published by Thorogood, London, 2004.

In some instances we have been unable to trace the owners of copyright material, and we would appreciate any information that would enable us to do so.

# Author's acknowledgements

There are many people who have contributed to the ideas in this book. Some of the case studies are taken directly from schools I have worked with while others are amalgams of situations in schools and conversations I have had with school leaders. The particular headteachers I would like to thank are:

Vicky Davies
Kate Slatcher
Debbie Quinn
Carolyn Banfield
Heather Dowding
Wendy Marriot
Rachel Edwards

I would also like to thank Gill Fowler, Maggie Garland, Candy Kerpache and Ray Tolhurst for their support and help.

# Preface

The main aim of this book is to provide an introduction to using coaching with staff in schools. If you are interested in coaching and how it can affect the learning of staff in terms of building their capacity, then this is the book for you. If you are someone who works in a school and you see yourself as a lifelong learner then you will find this book to be a powerful learning tool.

This book can help your professional development by giving you some tools for you to use in school, perhaps with the staff you lead or for use with a partner teacher. After reading this book on any level you will find that your interpersonal skills will improve, bringing elements of coaching into almost every conversation that you have.

Another aim of this highly practical book is to bring coaching to life. It is steeped in real schools and talks about current and up-to-date situations. The case studies and coaching conversations are all relevant to today's schools and the reader will be able to identify with many of them.

## Who is this book aimed at?

The audience for this book is a wide one. It is aimed at many different types of people working in a school. If you are leading a subject area then it will be of use to you in bringing people on board with the developments that you are trying to lead. It will also be good for your professional development and will build your leadership capacity.

If you are a team leader in school the book will be very useful in helping to build up your team and in developing your own leadership skills. Coaching provides a new and different framework for team working. It fits well with team development and provides a fresh approach towards getting the best from your team.

If you are responsible for the professional development of some staff or have a performance management role then the book can help you on a number of counts. It provides a useful framework for performance management, giving the responsibility to the learners for their own development. It also shows a cost-effective way of embedding the professional development of staff.

If you are a headteacher then there are many applications of this book. It can help you build a coaching culture within your school and develop the leadership capacity of all the staff. It can give you some new strategies for leading teams. The book will show how to share and distribute leadership within your school effectively and in a meaningful way.

Finally, if you believe in the capacity of people in a school to grow and learn then this book will resonate with you. So, read on.

## How to use this book

You will not learn to coach by just reading about it. This book is intended to be a practical guide to coaching within the context of a school. There are many ideas and techniques for you to try out. It contains many features to help with your learning.

**Key points** – This feature flags up a really important point. It will need you to think further at this point and reflect on what is being said.

**Coaching conversations** – This feature is designed to let you see what coaching looks like. The conversations are practical examples taken from the author's work as a coach in schools.

**Case studies** – These will be longer than coaching conversations and will give more detail about the context for the coaching sessions. They are more in-depth than the coaching conversations and are examples of good practice.

**Learning reviews** – These are at the end of each chapter and will give you a chance to reflect on and embed your learning and make notes of what you need to do next.

**Chapter summaries and chapter objectives** – These are intended to guide you through the chapters reminding you what we have covered and reinforcing the learning.

PREFACE

# Planning your route through the book

You are probably wondering which chapters are the most relevant to you. It clearly depends on how much time you have got, but following is a pragmatic chapter guide to help you navigate your way around the book.

Chapter 1 – What is coaching?

Chapter 2 – The essential skills of coaching

Chapter 3 – The coaching process

These first three chapters need to read by everyone. They provide a rationale for coaching and practical advice for building up your coaching skills. They also cover how to hold a coaching session.

Chapter 4 – How to develop a coaching culture in your school

This chapter will be useful for anyone who wants to introduce coaching to their team or whole school. Principally to be read be anyone in a leadership role in a school.

Chapter 5 – Coaching to make a difference

This chapter is of interest to everyone working in a school. It deals with coaching in a paired situation and some of the scenarios can be adapted to working with children as a learning mentor.

Chapter 6 – Coaching and performance management

This chapter is a useful guide for anyone who line manages other staff and who carries out performance management interviews. It will also be of interest to someone who is being performance managed and who feels they need to take more responsibility and ownership of the process.

Chapter 7 – Coaching and middle leadership

This chapter is for anyone who is leading a subject or an area in school. It is also of importance to anyone who line manages people with subject leadership responsibilities.

PREFACE

### Chapter 8 – Coaching and strategic development

This chapter is for anyone who is involved in deciding on the strategic direction of a whole school, subject or department.

### Chapter 9 – Coaching the team

This chapter will be of use to those people working in a school with some sort of team leadership responsibility. It will also be helpful to those leaders who are hoping to develop the leadership skills of their team leaders.

### Chapter 10 – Coaching and distributed leadership

This chapter will be of interest to those school leaders who are interested in coaching as a leadership style and who want a more devolved leadership structure within their school or department.

Now plan your route.

Use the following framework to reflect on and consider how you are going to use this book.

| |
|---|
| What do I want to achieve by reading this book? |
| What do I know about coaching already? |
| What do I need to find out about coaching? |
| Which chapters will I skim? |

# PREFACE

| |
|---|
| Which chapters will I study in depth? |
| |

| |
|---|
| When do I hope to have finished this by? |
| |

Congratulations, you have just had your first introduction to coaching by using a coaching framework to plan your study.

# 1

# What is coaching?

## This chapter in short

Most people have heard of coaching in a sporting or even a business context. This chapter will put coaching in an educational context and more especially in a context to be used by schools. Anyone in schools who has had to mentor, or been involved in inducting or training staff, will have touched on coaching and faced the challenge of doing it properly. This chapter highlights the different settings in which coaching can be used and makes clear how coaching can be a part of the professional development of all staff.

## Objectives

When you have completed this chapter you will be able to:

- understand what coaching is;
- realise the applications coaching has for schools as organisations;
- understand the relationship between coaching and mentoring;
- see how coaching can help you in your role at school;
- describe the benefits of coaching;
- identify areas where elements of coaching are already taking place at your school and build on them.

## The origins of coaching

Coaching has been used in business for years. It is commonplace for executives to have a coach. According to a survey by the Chartered Management Institute (http://www.managers.org.uk) 80 per cent of executives think that they would benefit from coaching and 96 per cent think coaching should be readily available to all employees. In the year 2000, the numbers of managers receiving coaching increased from 58 per cent in 1996 to 77 per cent.

Coaching is also growing in popularity and credibility in schools. It fits in well with the national agenda of personalised learning and distributed leadership. Coaching someone one to one, to an agenda that he/she has defined according to his/her needs, is the ultimate tool in personalised learning. Coaching also suits schools because it will be complimentary to the mentoring that is already happening.

Coaching is now at the heart of many leadership programmes coming from the National College for School Leadership (NCSL). 'Leading from the Middle' is an NCSL programme for middle leaders in schools that uses a model in which all the middle leaders on the programme have a leadership coach. The consultant leader programme, also from NCSL, for established school leaders, uses a coaching model to encourage school leaders to work collaboratively and learn from each other. 'The Primary Strategy', an initiative from the Department for Education and Skills (DfES) aimed at raising standards, relies heavily on coaching principles. Indeed the Training and Development Agency (TDA) think of coaching as so important that every new head is encouraged to employ a coach under the 'Headteachers' Induction Programme'.

Once you have learned both the skills and the structure of coaching you will begin to use it in most interactions you have at work. You will find it will come into your relationship with pupils, and your dealings with parents and the staff that you manage. Both the skills and framework of coaching have so many benefits at all levels of school life. Let us begin to get more specific and look at some of the applications of coaching in schools.

## The benefits of coaching

The benefits of using coaching in schools are many. Here are some for you to consider.

# WHAT IS COACHING?

- Coaching can accelerate the personal and professional development of staff.
- Coaching can help to retain staff.
- Coaching will help staff adapt to new roles or tasks.
- Coaching enhances team morale.
- Coaching is good at generating responsibility on the part of the learner.
- Coaching can accelerate the personal and professional development of staff.
- Coaching will underpin and help the implementation of organisational change.
- Coaching will support senior managers in their sometimes lonely role, offering a combination of challenge and support.
- Coaching will embed training so that it is more cost-effective.

## So what is coaching?

Coaching is a way of working alongside someone, giving him/her an opportunity to set goals and the support to achieve them. Not only will the coach help the learner work towards new goals, he/she will also affirm what is already being done. How often do we miss out this essential part of developing people?

People need to know what they are doing well so that they can carry on doing it. Other staff need to know what someone is doing well so that it can be shared and replicated in other classrooms. One of the key elements of sustained school improvement is consistent sharing of good practice. This can only take place if the good practice has been identified and praised first. There is no member of staff who does not enjoy being successful – so let them know! We can see for ourselves how this strategy works with children and as teachers we try really hard to praise pupils. Let us do it to our staff.

However, letting people know what they are doing well is only half the story. Coaching needs to focus on areas that the learner has identified as needing development.

So, the focus of each coaching session is on the person being coached (who I shall refer to as a 'learner') and will be future focused, centring on improving an area of work.

Here is a working definition of coaching:

*Coaching is a highly structured way of working one to one with an individual through a series of meetings. The coach will enable the learner to take responsibility for his/her learning, develop an awareness of his/her situation and increase his/her skills. It is a way of realising the potential of staff.*

The coach will hold the learner accountable for actions, which they both agree. It is not a cosy chat in which the learner offloads his/her problems and then feels better. It is a rigorous process, which will make demands on both the coach and learner. Through skilled questioning, the coach will ensure that the learner comes up with solutions and suggestions. Coaching is not about analysing what has gone before and what went wrong. It is totally focused on the future and makes the learner responsible for what happens. The coach should centre the development on the person being coached. The learner will be helped to diagnose the area of need that they need to develop. The coach may offer theories or models to employ and the learner is free to reject or work with these. Essentially, the coach stays within the learner's frame of reference and his/her own understanding of the area.

## Coaching and sport

Many teachers may have experience of coaching through the medium of sport. You may already be a coach or have received coaching in a particular one. You may have received or carry out coaching so much that it is second nature to you.

What do we mean by coaching in a non-sporting context, moreover in a workplace and, more especially, school context?

Well let's go back to sport for a moment. A sports coach will explain the rules of the sport, demonstrate the skills, watch those skills being practised, praise what is being done well, and give tips on how to improve. There are many parallels between this coaching approach and the one that I am going to explore. You know from teaching that children learn most effectively from a combination of demonstration, explanation of theory, a chance to put that theory into practice, getting feedback from the teacher and coaching.

Although all adults will have their own individual learning style, they will learn most effectively from active experimentation, encouragement and from having someone support them. A school that has a culture of coaching will encourage staff to take risks and experiment. If every member of staff is being coached and is coaching others, they will all feel encouraged and supported to try out new ideas. You can do this as a coach.

Not that coaching is all about being soft and fluffy.

Coaching is also about challenge. Powerful learning can take place when people are challenged to reflect and analyse their actions, in a supportive way. A coach can do this for you.

Time in school is at a premium. Pace dictates that there is very little time for reflection. Coaching will build in that time in a structured way to ensure that personal learning is reviewed. It can also provide a framework for teams to think about where they are. Coaching will pose the right questions and facilitate the deep learning that goes beneath the surface to enable a deep sustainable personal growth that will last. Thus, coaching supports both staff development and school improvement.

To illustrate this point the following is a quote from Kate Slatcher, a headteacher who has just introduced coaching into her school:

> Coaching is giving us the time to develop as individuals and professionals. In a school you need to be able to trust your colleagues and coaching develops this trust. Coaching is developing our team as we recognise the value of supporting each other. In our school, coaching is opening up a professional dialogue, allowing people to seek help without feeling inadequate. Learning is a continuous process and coaching is a way of enabling our adults as well as our children to enjoy learning.

## A coaching culture

A school with a coaching culture is one where there is no such thing as failure. Imagine how different your professional life would be if you did not feel the fear of failure. Think about what it would be like if you worked in a school where all the staff was so confident that if things went wrong there would be no retribution or comeback. If you have staff who are being coached and are coaching each other you will build up a totally supportive staff that share and celebrate each other's diverse talents and skills. That is not to say that everything will go well all of the time.

### KEY POINT

In a school with a coaching culture, mistakes are just seen as an inevitable part of the change process. They are treated lightly rather than being dwelt upon and analysed. What is capitalised on in these schools is the learning that comes from this process.

Whatever role you have in school, if you are being coached you will feel supported enough to develop your own talents and skills using them for the benefit of the children in your care.

Staff who see the benefit of coaching and are coaching each other as a matter of course will also be able to adapt and change more easily. The one thing that everyone in education knows is that the change is here to stay and the pace of change is getting faster. Whether it is changes in the examination system, the curriculum or teachers' pay and conditions, there is always going to be change and innovation. A school that is using coaching regularly will be able to adapt easily to changes and also be confident enough to retain that which they value for the good of the pupils.

On the subject of pupils, what will be the benefit for them of using coaching in schools?

The coaching model we will examine can be adapted for use with pupils. In most schools the aims and values usually contain one about developing a child's true potential – that is what coaching is all about.

Coaching can be used to help pupils carry out target setting and define their own learning goals. It can also help children with limiting beliefs, such as low self-esteem, work on those areas that are holding them back. Both these areas will enhance learning and encourage them to be independent and reflective learners.

## Recap

So, coaching is about:

- nurturing the development of the individual;
- challenging the learner;
- offering an opportunity for reflection;
- creating a climate for developing people;
- establishing staff who are flexible and adaptable to change;
- eliminating blocks to learning.

# The applications of coaching in schools

Further chapters in the book will cover the various applications of coaching in the school context. As you become more familiar with coaching you will think of many more. To begin with here are some of the more obvious ones:

- performance management interviews;
- cascading training;
- implementing initiatives, i.e. curriculum;
- moving teams forward;
- forming new teams;
- managing difficult parents;
- behaviour management;
- inducting new members of staff;
- problem solving;
- working with the school's council;
- sharing knowledge and expertise.

Whatever the situation, the set of skills developed for coaching is the same. Once learned, they will only improve with practice, so it is really important to build them into the culture of your school and your everyday work.

Two contexts in which coaching is used in schools are the coaching of both individuals and teams.

Individuals can be coached by either a senior member of staff or peer, depending on the circumstances. Individuals would be coached by another individual on a one-to-one basis. This may form part of a mentoring programme or part of the performance management process. These sessions would be confidential and there would be a balance of personal development and school improvement matters. Coaching teams would be led by someone outside that team, who had been trained in coaching skills. By coaching a team it moves forward and out of a phase of its development that it may be stuck in.

Individual coaching sessions can:

- improve teacher performance in the classroom;
- increase someone's job satisfaction and work–life balance;
- close that gap between where someone is now and where they want to be;
- solve problems that staff are stuck on and improve the way they manage change;

- improve staff skills in delegation and performance management;
- help everyone manage the many stresses of the job;
- renew zest and commitment to teaching, which innovation-weary teachers may have lost.

Team coaching can:

- renew a team's goals and firm up its direction;
- give a framework to tackle change;
- release the team's potential;
- reduce conflict, which may be holding them back;
- cascade training;
- ensure more effective communication between team members.

These days it is essential that schools find ways of promoting staff working collaboratively, making maximum use of the limited amount of time that is available. Staff who are used to being coached and using coaching skills with each other will be able to solve their own problems, develop skills and rely less on outside consultants to find solutions to difficulties that may arise.

## Coaching and mentoring – similarities and differences

Schools will already be familiar with the process of mentoring. Staff may have had experience of being newly qualified teacher (NQT) mentors or mentors to student teachers. Experienced heads may have been asked to mentor new headteachers. New staff joining a school may have been allocated a mentor. Indeed, as the table opposite indicates, coaching and mentoring have a lot in common. If you have been a mentor you will be already well on the way to understanding what coaching is.

In terms of skills set that are needed for a successful coach to operate well a good mentor will already have some of these.

The table opposite makes clear the overlap between coaching and mentoring, and the common elements between the two processes. Mentoring will take place over a prolonged period of time, maybe even a year. Someone new to a job or a role will have a mentor. Within that time, the mentor may carry out coaching sessions or adopt a coaching technique. Clearly there are huge overlaps between coaching and mentoring in terms of the process and skills involved from the coach or mentor.

# WHAT IS COACHING?

| Coaching | Mentoring |
|---|---|
| **Similarities** | |
| ■ Based on a series of one-to-one discussions | |
| ■ Need a relationship between individuals that is based on trust | |
| ■ Rely on confidentiality being maintained by both parties | |
| ■ Both the mentee and learner grow in confidence | |
| ■ Both the coach and mentor respect each other | |
| ■ Need dedicated time defined for regular sessions | |
| ■ Both mentees and learners are often keen to go on and act as coaches and mentors | |
| ■ Help the school to grow its own experts by investing in and developing staff | |
| ■ Improve the climate of collaborative working within a school | |
| ■ Improve the skill of the person offering coaching and mentoring as well as those on the receiving end | |
| ■ Engender strong working relationships between members of staff | |
| ■ Build on and develop the skills of the learner and mentee | |

While being a mentor is a valuable experience for the new coach to build on, the coach needs to realise that it is not the same process and a complimentary skills set is required.

Coaching and mentoring are very different and the differences are both subtle and obvious.

| Coaching | Mentoring |
|---|---|
| **Differences** | |
| ■ Coaches do not readily give advice on specific ways of working | ■ Freely gives hints and tips on how they have tackled situations |
| ■ Do not need to have carried out the specific role of the learner in school | ■ Will have had the same role as the mentees at some point in their careers |
| ■ Will use a structured model for their conversations with agreed outcomes | ■ Can give quick-fix solutions or ideas |
| ■ The agenda focus is on drawing out the latent skills of the learner | ■ Although sometimes meetings follow a structure, there is much informal mentoring contact |
| ■ Rely on learners to come up with their own answers and generate their own questions | ■ The focus is on passing on knowledge from an experienced member of staff to an inexperienced one |

COACHING FOR SCHOOLS

| Coaching | Mentoring |
|---|---|
| ■ The process relies on a technique of skilled questions from the coach to move the process forward<br>■ Can sometimes focus on a narrow skill set | ■ Will be a long-term assignment concerning the whole role of the mentee |

As the table above illustrates, one of the differences between coaching and mentoring lies in the roles of the coach and learner. The learner must take total responsibility for meeting goals and carrying out actions.

In a mentoring session the mentee, say an NQT, may ask the mentor for some ideas on a particular area, i.e. planning lessons. The mentor may respond by digging out some planning he/she has done and give it to the mentee as examples. The mentor may also lend or show the mentee some examples of resources he/she has used in a particular lesson. Coaching can be used to address specific issues and can form part of a mentoring programme.

A coaching conversation on, for example, the area of planning may take place as part of a mentoring programme. In this example, the NQT mentor is using coaching as part of her work to support the NQT.

## Coaching conversation

*Jane, a Year 4 teacher, has seemed unusually tired and her mentor has noticed that her planning has not been handed in on time. This is unusual for Jane. In the staffroom she has mentioned to others that she is bogged down by planning and completely overwhelmed. The school is using QCA documents supplemented by a Published Math's scheme for planning. There are two statemented pupils in Jane's class and a further 15 per cent of pupils who are working below expected levels.*

*Jane's mentor brings up the subject of planning in one of the regular mentoring sessions and uses a coaching framework to explore the issue.*

COACH: You have mentioned that planning is not going too well.

JANE: Yes, I just can't get my head around it, there is so much to cover. I am spending hours on it. I just can't seem to cover it all: the differentiation, the assessment element, the next steps, the objectives, the statemented kids with their Individual Education Plans (IEPs). I don't

## WHAT IS COACHING?

|||
|---|---|
| | know where to start. I have my Planning, Preparation and Assessment (PPA) time and my non-contact and it just seems to disappear. |
| COACH: | So you're feeling overwhelmed by planning for your class? |
| JANE: | Yes. I feel am no good at any of it. |
| COACH: | Out of all of the elements you mentioned, which one is giving you the most problems? |
| JANE: | All of it, it's all a complete mess. |
| COACH: | So, describe this mess to me. What actually happens when you plan? |
| JANE: | Well, I use the school's format and I start with the lesson objectives and then I have to think of an activity – the scheme of work is quite good for that. Then I get stuck on how to differentiate; I just can't seem to think of anything. |
| COACH: | When you say differentiate, do you mean for the Special Educational Needs (SEN) pupils or for the more able? |
| JANE: | Well it's really the less able because the scheme of work has extension activities for the top group. |
| COACH: | So, what is actually happening when you plan is that you are getting stuck on the differentiation for lower ability pupils. |
| JANE: | Yes, that's what is getting me down. I feel that there are so many of them in the class and they get disruptive if there's not enough work planned for them, and if the work is too hard. |
| COACH: | So, what could you do about this? |
| JANE: | I am not sure. I don't know. |
| COACH: | Just have a think about it, what could you do? If you were advising a friend, what would you tell him/her? |
| JANE: | I would tell him/her to go and ask for help. I suppose I could do that I could ask the Special Educational Needs Coordinator (SENCO). I could try to arrange to plan with someone just for the SEN kids. I could try to get some fresh ideas. |

You can see at once the subtle questioning of the coach that led to Jane identifying her own problem and area to work on.

The coach resisted the temptation to say: 'When I had your year group I did it like this' or 'What you should be doing is . . .'.

Instead the coach managed to get Jane to focus on what was actually happening when she planned, rather than what she thought was happening. Also, another point to note when discussing the skill of the coach in this particular example, is the way in which the coach is completely unphased when he asked the learner to identify the area giving the most difficulty and the learner replied that it was all a mess. The temptation may have been to sympathise and say 'I am sure it's not that bad, you must be doing something right'. Instead, through skillful questioning, the coach managed to get Jane to identify the elements that were going well and what the problem areas were. Having identified what the problem is themselves, learners will be much more likely to come up with a sustainable solution.

You will also notice that the coach reflected back and summarised what the learner had said.

Coaching, by its nature, is a learner-centred activity. It is essential, therefore, to clarify the roles of the learner and the coach from the outset. An agreement needs to be reached, making explicit what the roles and expectations of both the coach and the learner are.

Before any coaching session can begin, a shared understanding needs to be agreed, setting out expectations of both the coach and the learner. An initial discussion needs to take place to outline the purpose of the coaching sessions.

## Clarifying expectations

In a coaching session it is important to be clear about what is expected from the coach or learner. The following case study illustrates a situation where a headteacher had decided that the staff would benefit from coaching without telling them.

### Case study

Name of school: Queensmount School

The coach was already coaching a headteacher who had brought her school out of special measures after a failed Ofsted inspection. Because of the circumstances of the school, the need for rapid improvement was essential. The head's leadership style, therefore, had been very top down, which involved ▶

telling the senior management teams what to do instead of consulting and developing them because of the constant pressure of visits from inspectors. After successfully coming out of special measures, the head wanted to change her style and make the team more proactive in its role, and she wanted the coach to coach them into taking a more high profile role in the leadership of the school. This was an exciting assignment and the coach was really eager to make a start. In fact in her eagerness she forgot a fundamental principle of coaching – clarifying expectations. The stage that she missed was the one in which the expectations of the people she was working with and that of the coach would be defined. She should have spent time clarifying what the purpose of the coaching sessions were before she started. The whole theme of the sessions should have started with a need, as perceived or identified by the members of the leadership team themselves. The trouble was that the senior management team had not been told by the head what the coach was intending to do and thought they were meeting her to follow up some other work that had been done on monitoring. This also involved another problem – the team did not know it needed coaching because it was not aware its performance needed improving. The coach should have spent some time discussing her role with the team and preparing the ground for her work. Instead she launched into the first session.

As a result of this situation, the coach spent the first session explaining what coaching was and what she hoped to achieve. Fortunately the coach had a strong relationship with the staff and was able to explain what they needed to work on. The coach could have avoided this situation if she had held a preliminary discussion with the team first and set some ground rules and explained what coaching was and why it was needed.

As well as the coach, the learner needs to understand what the coaching both is and is not. It is important to explain that coaching is not counselling or therapy. It is important to explain the nature of coaching and that results are not guaranteed. The learner needs to know that he/she is responsible for creating his/her own results. The coach's role will have to be explained – a coach is there to guide, support and motivate.

## KEY POINT

**The role of the coach is to help the learner achieve his/her goals and assist in achieving his/her potential, not to tell him/her what to do.**

This is sometimes difficult when the expectation of the learner is for the coach to solve his/her problems. A phrase often heard by coaches is: 'You're a life coach, great. You know how to sort out my life, now tell me what to do.'

## Coaching, not telling

In education, the difference between consulting and coaching needs to be made clear, especially if you are working in both capacities on separate assignments. If you are acting as a coach you will not be telling the learner what to do and therefore will not be providing any quick and easy solutions. If you are acting as a consultant, you may well be telling the schools what to do and giving them your advice based on your experience and professional expertise. There are many drawbacks to this.

Telling involves having all the answers; it usually takes the shape of identifying a problem and calling in an expert to come up with the answers. Of course, there is a role for the consultant and expert to play. If the ICT suite breaks down then you will need an expert to solve it, or maybe an ICT consultant to identify the problem. In other words, someone with a specialised knowledge who will provide answers and fix the ICT suite, whose role is to fix it and then leave. If it happens again, then you have to call that expert in again. To some extent, you build up a dependency on that expert: he/she has skills and expertise that you do not, so it is these that you pay for.

However, there are many situations and problems in schools that could be solved using a coaching approach. If you use a coaching approach you may need the help of a coach but you will not be relying on that person. A coach can help by working with you so that you are building up your own skills. A consultant or expert will presume that he/she knows what is best for the school. A coach will assume that the people in the school have the answers. Coaching is based on the belief that people are full of potential and their own answers lie inside them; the job of the coach and the coaching process is to unlock that potential and those answers.

As we saw in the earlier coaching conversation, telling the NQT what to do about planning would provide an attractive, quick and easy solution to the problem. However, it would have disempowered the NQT and encouraged her to come to the coach every time she had a problem. Coaching, rather than telling, will increase the teacher's confidence and engender longer-term benefits. The coach needs to explain that the benefits of coaching are far more sustainable than

# WHAT IS COACHING?

those of telling. In education, school leaders are under enormous pressure from the government and Local Authorities (LAs) so there has been a tendency to rely on consultants to provide answers. Coaching will encourage school leaders to 'grow' their own answers.

As we saw earlier, it is important to resist pressure from the learner to rush into problem solving because, unless you decide where you are going from the outset, you will not be able to measure progress and record results. It may be helpful to look at this table to clarify expectations of the coach and learner. Each school will need to draw one of these up as befits its situation but here are some suggestions.

The expectations of the coach and learner are as follows.

| Coach | Learner |
| --- | --- |
| ■ To be non-judgemental | ■ To keep appointments |
| ■ To keep appointments | ■ To carry out agreed actions in between sessions |
| ■ To give the learner his/her full attention | ■ To 'be there' fully during sessions in terms of concentration |
| ■ To provide coaching tools/ frameworks when helpful | ■ To accept full responsibility for the situation and to carry out agreed actions |
| ■ To maintain confidentiality | |
| ■ To keep notes when necessary | |
| ■ To believe in the learner's capability to move forward | |

## Accepting responsibility

This is something that is key to the coaching process. In order to move forward, with either an issue or a development point, the learner must accept responsibility for his/her own progress.

People often have a tendency to either blame someone or something else for their problems. It is easy to blame the LA, Department for Education (DfES), headteacher, awkward member of staff, for your demise: we have all done it. However, we can only change ourselves, not other people, so that is an important message for the coach to put over. Here's a coaching conversation to illustrate the point.

## Coaching conversation

Mark is a young and inexperienced year head in a large secondary school.

COACH: So what is the issue you would like to discuss?

MARK: It's about my role as Year 8 team leader; it's not going well, in fact I am having real problems.

COACH: Tell me more.

MARK: Well it's Mrs Smith, she is completely undermining me. Every time I give out deadlines she misses them. She was the last one to bring me the grades for parents' evening; she arrives late for year group meetings. Every time I speak to her she says she will improve but she never does. She really is the weak link in the team. She does not set an example to the other team members. I really don't know what to do. I have tried everything and nothing works. She really is bringing me down. Without her it is such a good team.

COACH: So you are really feeling she is not pulling her weight?

MARK: Yes, that's it in a nutshell.

COACH: Well what are you trying to achieve here?

MARK: I really want her to leave, the whole year group is suffering because of her – she won't be told. There's nothing that I can do with her. The team is not going to move forward with her in it. There's no point in anything I do with her around. She is affecting my relationship with everyone else in the team. I really can't move forward and achieve my own targets with her around.

COACH: Do you think her moving on is a possibility?

MARK: Yes, I think so. She keeps on complaining that she has a terrible journey in to work and that she has to leave too early in the morning. I know she has been looking for jobs nearer home. If only she could apply and get one, everything would be all right.

Here the coach has made a mistake and it is an easy trap to fall into. The issue of whether or not Mrs Smith will move on is a red herring and not relevant to the development of the skills of Mark. The coach should be focusing on developing the year head's leadership skills by getting him to think of strategies to deal with Mrs Smith, not encouraging him to centre the conversation on whether Mrs Smith will leave or not. The point is, there will always be Mrs Smiths and the team leader needs to develop his skills of leading difficult people rather than getting Mrs Smith a new post!

The coach's main task here is to make Mark realise that Mrs Smith is not being coached but the team leader is. The session needs to centre on what the team leader can do to change the limiting belief that Mrs Smith holds the key to the team's future. It will probably take a few sessions of careful questioning to move the year head forward from thinking that Mrs Smith is the source of all his problems.

## Coaching and future thinking

Unlike counselling or therapy, coaching is totally focused on the future. It does not need to unpick what has gone on before in terms of what went wrong. Some teams and individuals find it difficult to move out of thinking about a golden era, when things were better.

> **KEY POINT**
>
> Coaching will focus on shaping the future and very much focuses on setting goals and defining actions.

Coaching is very much a two-way process and there are benefits both for the coach and the learner. The learner can become a more reflective practitioner through coaching. If the coach is a senior member of the staff, it can be very illuminating to see the institution through the eyes of an NQT or new teacher. In schools, a lot of attention is given to mentoring and coaching newly appointed teachers. Teachers already have had training and this is followed up with mentoring in their first year. New headteachers now arrive at school with the National Professional Qualification for Headship (NPQH). However, how much coaching do we give to newly appointed team leaders in school? How much coaching and mentoring do we give to new admin assistants or to people within school who have taken on a new role and responsibilities? This is where coaching can help. Very often there is so much expertise and potential within a school, and a lot of it goes unnoticed. A school that uses coaching regularly will grow its own leaders and thoroughly induct new staff.

## Coaching and staff development

> **KEY POINT**
>
> Careful coaching can build skills in staff and develop them in a sustainable way, and make training a process rather than an event.

Coaching comes in not only when staff take on new roles but also when they have new tasks. For instance, a new Foundation Stage leader may find him-/herself giving a presentation to new parents for the first time. A new deputy head may find him-/herself in charge of the school for the first time and may need coaching on what to expect, a new head of department may have to do lesson observations for the first time and will need coaching sessions on how to give feedback.

Sometimes people in schools are promoted internally to more senior positions without any proper coaching or mentoring in their new role. They are simply meant to assume that role without any proper support. An example of good practice in this area is a school that builds coaching sessions in to an induction programme for staff who take on new roles. By asking the right questions and holding a structured series of coaching sessions, rather than telling someone how to do it, a coach can help develop specific skills in new areas.

## Coaching and continued professional development

Some schools employ a system of disseminating knowledge from courses through reporting back at staff meetings, but how effective is that and what impact does it make on those who hear it? There must be many people who ask themselves how cost-effective is the type of staff development activity that sends a member of staff out to a course and then relies on him/her to disseminate his/her learning back at school. The most sustainable In-Service Education and Training (INSET) is one that takes a coaching approach to staff development.

A successful model to base INSET on should involve an initial input from the trainer or lead coach in the subject, followed up by a number of coaching sessions. The coaching sessions should involve a discussion on how the new initiative is going and an opportunity to share good practice or identify common problems. A school that has a coaching culture may have already established coaching pairs of staff who could work in this way. Alternatively, after the initial training, the school may identify a lead coach as a member of staff who is going

# WHAT IS COACHING?

to work closely with other staff on whatever the area of development was. The lead coach may have received some extra training in the area that the school is working on.

Sustainable learning on the part of staff will not happen through INSET, unless people get the chance to practise new skills and be coached on them. The professional development of staff has to be tackled in a systematic way with coaching at its centre. A model of training and developing staff could be adopted whereby any new initiative is explained to staff and then they coach each other on it.

For instance, if the school was working on developing thinking skills. The whole school could train all staff in an area and then a member of staff could be appointed as coach in that particular area and be given some extra training. The coach would then hold regular review sessions with individuals to reflect and review progress. In order to bring about sustainable change it is necessary to visit new learning more than once. If we want to facilitate that deep leaning, as discussed earlier, a cycle of training review and reflection needs to be adapted to any new initiative or system that the school is adopting.

Below is a model that may be useful when carrying out staff development or training.

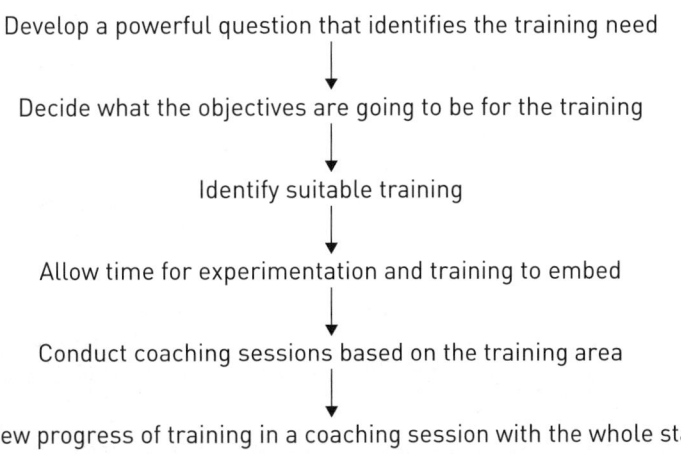

A case study will illustrate this model further.

## Case study

A 250-place primary school, in a socially deprived area of Weston-super-Mare in Somerset, was having problems with behaviour management. There was a history of using assertive discipline at the school but this had been introduced five years ago and a lot of staff had changed since then. Both the head and the staff knew that there was something wrong with the discipline at the school but were not quite sure what to do, as abandoning the assertive discipline policy after it had worked so well in the past, did not seem right. Lately there had been some instances of very disruptive behaviour by some pupils. Staff felt challenged by the inclusion agenda and were having to cope with a number of children with complex emotional and behavioural difficulties who previously would have been statemented or in a special school. The school up until recently had been renowned for its good discipline and it was a good feature in its Ofsted report of a year ago.

Here's how the staff tackled the situation using the above model.

Develop a powerful question that identifies the problem
↓
*How do we improve behaviour management at the school in a way that upholds the principles of assertive discipline?*
↓
Decide what the objectives are going to be for the training
- *To re-establish what we mean by assertive discipline*
- *To train all staff in implementing it*
- *To review our system of using it*
- *To make amendments to old system of applying assertive discipline or invent new one*

↓
Identify suitable training
*Employ services of educational psychology staff to conduct INSET with all staff (support staff and teachers)*
↓
Allow time for experimentation and training to embed
*Pair up staff into coaching buddies and allow time for them to swap successes and failures with the implementation (over six months)*
↓
Conduct coaching sessions based on the training area
*Experienced member of staff who has received further training from educational psychology staff becomes the behaviour coach and holds coaching sessions with coaching buddy pairs*
↓
Review progress of training in a coaching session with the whole staff
*Hold full staff meeting facilitated by the behaviour coach to establish the next powerful question*

# WHAT IS COACHING?

We could fill this book with definitions of coaching, but, essentially, I see it as a process that facilitates the learning and development of the learner. To be a coach you need to understand the process and practise the skills that we will explore in Chapter Two.

> **Chapter summary**
>
> - Coaching enables staff to develop their full potential.
> - Coaching embeds professional development.
> - A school that uses coaching avoids a culture of failure.
> - There are subtle differences between coaching and mentoring although they share a number of skill sets.
> - Through coaching, staff come up with their own solutions to problems.

## Your learning in practice

### Exercise

1. What is your definition of coaching? What do you understand by the term coaching?

| What do you understand as coaching? | How are you going to use it? |
|---|---|
|  |  |

COACHING FOR SCHOOLS

2. Think for a moment of your school and its individual and unique context. List all the staff development activities that go on, both informal and formal. How many of these activities already contain elements of coaching? How many of them would benefit from a coaching element? Use the template below, and include all teaching and non-teaching staff, and include any activity that aims to develop staff.

| Professional development activity | Member of staff | Contains elements of coaching |
|---|---|---|
|  |  |  |
|  |  |  |
|  |  |  |
|  |  |  |

3. Think of the way in which you approach staff development. How could you use a series of coaching questions to bring more reflection into the process?

| Professional development area | Training objectives | Coaching sessions | Evaluation of training through coaching session |
|---|---|---|---|
|  |  | Who? When? | Who? When? |
|  |  |  |  |
|  |  |  |  |
|  |  |  |  |

WHAT IS COACHING?

# Learning review

In terms of the areas listed below what are your key learning points?
What do you need to do now, in terms of further reading, discussions with staff and trying ideas out, to embed that learning?
Plan what you are going to do within the next month and put time aside to do it.

| Coaching development plan | | |
|---|---|---|
| Reading | Discussion with staff | Experimenting |
| What? When? | | |
| | | |
| | | |
| | | |

# 2
# The essential skills of coaching

## This chapter in short

This chapter identifies the three main building blocks of coaching. It explains in detail the skills involved in these building blocks, and provides examples and case studies for you to embed your learning. It also provides a context and a framework for the building blocks.

## Objectives

When you have completed this chapter you will be able to:

- identify the key skills needed to become a coach;
- name the coaching skills you are already proficient at;
- carry out a skills audit to see which skills you need to develop;
- build up a bank of useful coaching questions;
- understand what is meant by rapport building, effective questioning and listening to learn.

## Who can be a coach?

It does not follow that just because you have a career in education you can be a coach. You will need to learn and practise new skills. If you are training all staff in the skills of coaching, you will need to include several skills workshops in your training programme. As someone with a background in teaching and learning, you will already have a leaning towards coaching. Your skill set may already be well stocked. If you have had experience in mentoring or counselling you will already have some measure of skill in the areas that coaching requires. However, there are discrete areas of skills that are required to be an effective coach and these need to be taught and practised regularly. A good coach will need a high level of competence in effective questioning, active listening and rapport-building. These skills are the building blocks of coaching.

## The building blocks of coaching

| Coaching building blocks | | |
| --- | --- | --- |
| Rapport-building | Listening for learning | Effective questioning |

### Rapport-building

Good rapport is when you feel comfortable with the person you are talking to. You feel understood and valued. Having rapport with someone is probably something you take for granted. You probably have never really analysed it in too much detail. People you have a good rapport with you feel at ease with. In all the daily interactions in our working lives, there are always people who we seem to open up to easily. There are others who you feel more guarded with. Some people you have a natural rapport with and others you may need to work at it. In order to establish a coaching relationship with someone you need to have a good rapport with them and building this up is a skill you can learn.

> **KEY POINT**
>
> At the heart of coaching is communication. Good levels of open communication can only take place if good rapport is established.

People who are skilled at building rapport do it naturally and intuitively, so that it is not noticeable. Analysing what makes up good rapport is difficult as it is something that is often felt rather than quantified. However, there are elements of a good rapport that can be examined.

The purpose of rapport-building is for the learner to feel at one with the coach, trusted and listened to. In order to establish this relationship of mutual trust the coach needs to learn how to speak the learner's language.

### *Learning to build rapport – the key elements*

#### *Language*

To create rapport with someone we need to study his or her style of language and try to match it. In other words, reflect back to them what they are saying in terms of style as well as content. This will make them feel valued and listened to. If a person feels valued then the communication is more likely to flow and the coaching session will be productive with the learner benefiting fully from the experience. Linguistic styles tend to fall into three basic types. These link to the three learning styles. Each learner will favour the particular linguistic style that is in tune with his or her learning style.

Anyone who has studied teaching and learning styles will recognise the three basic styles of learning:

- visual;
- auditory;
- kinaesthetic.

Learners with a predominance of one of these styles will use particular words and phrases that indicate their learning and linguistic preference.

People with a visual style may use phrases like:

- 'I see what you mean'.
- 'Show me what you mean'.
- 'I see what you are saying'.
- 'For me that looks good'.
- 'I get the picture'.

People with an auditory preference may say things like:

- 'I hear what you are saying.'
- 'I am listening to what you say.'

- 'That sounds like a good idea.'
- 'That's as clear as a bell.'

People with a kinaesthetic preference will use phrases like:

- 'I felt comfortable'.
- 'That really touched me'.
- 'I was feeling really low at the time'.
- 'I cannot grasp this'.

By matching a person's linguistic style and literally using their language you will be in rapport with them. You will therefore be able to communicate with them more effectively. The learner will be using the one of the three senses that they have already developed to a high degree to communicate with you; it will be their natural way of speaking. You will need to observe their preferred style of communicating to be able to match it.

As well as the type of language someone uses, the tempo and tonality of their voice can also be matched. Visual people tend to talk very quickly, they can actually see what they are talking about and are in a rush to communicate this. They may jump from one topic to another because they can see the link between the two and are oblivious that to others there is no link. They literally talk in pictures and can get frustrated when others don't see them as clearly as they do.

Auditory people tend to talk with a rhythmic tone, maybe in a musical style. They like to explain themselves in a sequential way. In contrast, kinaesthetic people like to talk very slowly and deliberately. They will need time to process their thoughts and there may be a lot of silences when they are explaining something. These silences are very important and it is essential for the coach not to interrupt, as the kinaesthetic learner will get very frustrated and the coach will close them down if he or she tries to fill those gaps with what the coach thinks the learner is trying to say.

You can immediately see why some staff meetings never seem to get anywhere. Imagine a room with three visual, three auditory and three kinaesthetic communicators in it. Each person will want to give his/her opinion and will need to be listened to. The three styles of communication are going to come into conflict when trying to come to a consensus.

When you are coaching someone they need to feel that you have empathy for them and that they are being listened to. The communication between the coach and learner needs to be free and unimpeded. This can only happen if the coach and learner are in rapport and rapport can be established with someone by mirroring their linguistic preference, speech tonality and body language.

COACHING FOR SCHOOLS

Remember the coaching session is not about the coach, the coach is not the expert with all the answers. The session is focused on the learner and his/her version of the world. How he/she sees the world will be communicated in the style of language, physiology and the tonality of his/her speech. By establishing rapport with the learner the coach can lead the learner through the coaching session to a successful outcome. This example will illustrate how rapport can be established, through matching someone's linguistic style.

### Coaching conversation

Kate, Tim's line manager, had a coaching session booked with Tim, head of Year 9, following the INSET they had had on the new pupil target-setting system that had been introduced. Kate had noticed that although Tim was a very able teacher, during the training day he seemed to have taken longer than the other staff to grasp new concepts. He seemed to be frustrated with the other staff, who he perceived as talking over him and ignoring his point. He did not generally feel listened to in staff meetings and yet his support for the new scheme was crucial to its success. Sometimes this feeling had led to problems and other staff saw him as difficult and, at times, holding the team back. Kate had noticed that his style of speech was a little pedestrian and she thought he was a kinaesthetic communicator. Kate opened the coaching session by asking how Tim thought that the training had gone.

TIM: I don't feel the day went very well at all. I felt left behind and, as always, there didn't seem to be enough time to make my points. As usual it's another rushed job... (pause). I just cannot get to grips with this target setting.... (pause) I can't get a feel of how it is going to work; to me it feels like a lot of extra work.

KATE: You are obviously not feeling very good about this. What would it take to make you feel positive towards it?

TIM: What would it take... (pause) mmm that's a good question. Maybe ... I just need time to get the feel of it. Maybe just try it out with a few kids first.

Kate carried on the session slowing down her own speech pattern to match Tim's tempo. By letting Tim pause and reflecting back the worries he had about the new system, mirroring his language and tone, she made him feel understood. Kate tried to see the world through Tim's glasses, rather than making him put hers on.

By the end of the half hour Tim was ready to proceed with a small pilot group of pupils.

THE ESSENTIAL SKILLS OF COACHING

> **Exercise**
>
> Pay attention to the next three conversations you have with people. Try to analyse the language that they used. Did the words they chose give any clue to their linguistic style? Did their language have any elements of visual, auditory or kinaesthetic patterns?

*Body language*

Another important aspect of rapport is body language. Research shows that 55 per cent of the meaning you derive from communicating with someone comes from their physiology, 38 per cent from the tone of voice and only 7 per cent comes from the words that they use. Sending out the right signals with your body language is fundamental to establishing a good coaching relationship. Getting the body language right as a coach can make a huge difference to how the session goes.

You may be someone who is intuitively skilled at building rapport. If not, like all aspects of coaching skills, rapport-building can be taught and gets better with practise.

You will able to judge whether or not you have a good rapport with someone just by how you feel when you are with them. Even if you know the person well and work with them, you may find that during a coaching session you have lost rapport with them. Maybe the situation is a little difficult or strained. This is the time to work on rapport-building through mirroring their body language. Have a look at them and their posture. Are they leaning forward? Are they using a lot of hand gestures?

By gently mirroring someone's body language, by copying their gestures, you can regain rapport, make them feel comfortable and above all understood. Obviously this has dangers and can get ridiculous. If you do not do it in a subtle way it could become a game in which the learner could feel that he/she is being made fun of. The trick is to do it without the learner realising that it is being done.

## COACHING FOR SCHOOLS

> ### Exercise
>
> In one of your coaching skills sessions, the following exercise will help you develop you rapport-building skills. In a pair, get the learner to speak for two minutes on how he/she came to be working where he/she is now and what have been the key highlights on the journey. The coach needs to just listen and make one or two comments, purely reflecting back the learner's main points. At this point the coach is to ask a few clarifying questions. When reflecting back, the coach should try to use the learner's language style and gently mirror the learner's body language.
>
> The learner then needs to report back to the coach on the following questions.
>
> - What did the coach do to make you feel understood?
> - Did anything the coach do interfere with the process?
> - What did the coach do that made you feel comfortable?
> - What did you notice about the process?

**Coaching building blocks**

Rapport-building   Listening for learning   Effective questioning

### Listening for learning

Listening is one of the cornerstones on which coaching is built. A rule of thumb in all coaching conversations is that the coach should only be doing 30 per cent of the talking. The coach, therefore, has a lot of listening to do. To be listened to effectively is a powerful experience for the learner. In this section we are going to explore what happens when we listen and what the listener actually does. We have all experienced talking to a poor listener. Not all of what the listener does is helpful. Here is a list of the less helpful behaviours and responses made by what we would call a bad listener:

- looks away;
- interrupts;
- finishes your sentences;
- offers you solutions without you asking;
- looks bored;

- fidgets;
- looks at his/her watch;
- asks too many questions;
- does most of the talking;
- gives you his/her opinion without asking.

Under times of stress we have all displayed some of these elements of a bad listener and yet we can all recall how frustrating it can be to be treated in this way. The learner will feel totally devalued and demotivated if not listened to properly.

> **KEY POINT**
>
> **The key purpose of listening in a coaching session is for the coach to understand the learner.**

The function of listening is not so that the coach can follow his/her own interest during the coaching conversation. It is not so that the coach can look sympathetic to the learner. It is so that the learner can lead the coach to a better understanding of his/her situation. When the learner explains his/her situation to the coach, he/she actually comes to a better understanding of it him-/herself.

Speaking and listening is a national curriculum subject that is taught in schools but how much time is actually spent on teaching listening rather than speaking? Teachers often complain that children do not know how to listen and it is easy to see how lack of listening can impede a child's progress in school.

It is often assumed that listening is a skill we teach children and we do not need to learn ourselves. However, there are different levels of listening and coaching requires a deep level of listening, which we call *listening for learning*. Listening for learning is a skill that can be practised and taught to staff through a variety of exercises in this chapter.

There are three different layers of listening and *listening for learning* is the deepest level. A good coach will be listening for learning.

Listening levels:

- surface listening;
- directed listening;
- listening for learning.

### Surface listening

This first level of listening is characterised by the listener giving off signals that he/she is listening, like nodding and smiling, but his/her mind is somewhere else. The listener is fully focused on him-/herself and his/her mind is processing the information taken in on a subconscious level. The listener, at this level, is forming in his/her mind the next response. The mind of the listener is wandering on to all sorts of topics . . . the next meeting . . . tomorrows' lesson.

### Directed listening

At this level the listener is making more of an effort. The listener is concentrating on making sense of what the other person says. The listener is digging around in his/her own experience for something to identify with so that he/she can interpret what is being heard. The listener is very much rooted in his/her own world.

### Listening for learning

A good coach will listen at the level of *listening for learning*. This level of listening will involve the listener in suspending his/her own judgement of what the speaker is saying. The listener will lose his/her own identity and focus totally on the learner. The good coach will use his/her intuition and hear what is not being said and what lies beneath what is being said.

> **Exercise**
>
> Next time you are in a conversation during the school day with someone, observe which style of listening you are employing. Also try to notice what level the other person is employing. When you have done this try to improve your level of listening in your next conversation.
>
> What were the barriers to listening for learning? Did any of the following 'interferences' get in the way?

### Interferences

- Boredom.
- Thinking about the next appointment/lesson.
- Daydreaming.

# THE ESSENTIAL SKILLS OF COACHING

- Seeing something going on at the other end of the corridor that distracted you.
- Thinking about how you ought to react to the other person.
- Forming opinions and value judgements about what the other person is saying.
- Impatience because he/she seems to be taking a roundabout way of telling you something.
- Stress due to lack of time.

We all have our favourite interferences that get in the way of listening for learning. The important thing is to be aware of them and try to develop techniques for dealing with them when we are coaching.

## Key skills

The key skills of listening for learning are:

- switching off your own inner dialogue;
- sending out the right signals through non-verbal signals;
- summarising;
- suspending your own judgement;
- showing empathy.

## Switching off your inner dialogue

One of the main challenges to the coach during a coaching session is to switch off his/her inner dialogue while listening. Your inner dialogue is the voice that goes on inside your head. It says 'I know exactly what they mean . . . that happened to me . . .'.

Your inner dialogue delves back into your own history and tries to relate the information you are hearing to your listening and your own past experiences. By doing this you are able to make sense of the new information more easily.

It is natural, when someone tells you something to find a hanger in your own past experience that you can hang the new information on. That helps you to understand it more easily. Often when we have been talking to someone about, say, a holiday in Rome, he/she replies by saying something like:

'Oh yes Rome, my friends went there, they had a great time. They stayed in a lovely hotel really near the centre . . .'.

COACHING FOR SCHOOLS

Then he/she goes on to talk about his/her friend's holiday and all you wanted to do was share your experiences. You go away from the conversation feeling frustrated and not listened to.

It is absolutely essential to switch off your inner dialogue when carrying out a coaching session and it is something that is difficult, but it comes with practice. The following is an example of when you may need to switch off that inner dialogue. The example shows someone who is so eager to relate what she is hearing to her own experience that she does not listen to learn.

### Coaching conversation

Gill, the headteacher, is holding a coaching session with Mark, the deputy head, on leading staff meetings.

GILL: So Mark, you wanted to have this session because the staff meeting that you led while I was out did not go well.

MARK: Well it did not go as planned.

GILL: Tell me about it.

MARK: Well they all went off at tangents, there was no conclusion, everyone was talking at once and there was really no finished product at the end of the meeting.

GILL: I know exactly what you mean, that happened to me when I first started running meetings.

MARK: I felt that we had departed from the agenda...

GILL: What you need to do is make sure that you stick to the agenda, have a time limit for each item and then at the end go over what you have all decided.

MARK: Actually I found it was a very productive and creative session... what I wanted to work on was a way of making more meetings more open and less rigid so that we have a free flow of ideas, but if you don't think that's appropriate.

Gill was very eager to relate Mark's experience to her own and to share with him the strategy that had worked for her. What transpired is that she did not 'know what he meant'. She did not bother to take the time to listen to Mark and find out what his thoughts and ideas were. Instead, she latched on to something she could identify with and had had experience of and told him what to do.

# THE ESSENTIAL SKILLS OF COACHING

Gill should have asked Mark to clarify the situation. Then he would have been able to explore that particular situation and understood, himself, what was going on.

*Non-verbal signs*

One of the things a coach can do to show the learner that the coach is listening is use non-verbal signs.

The coach needs to actively listen and send off all those body language signals that give the learner positive messages that he/she is being listened to and valued. Active listening will consist of keeping eye contact with the learner, nodding, smiling and keeping body language open. The following is a listening exercise, which you may like to include in your coaching skills workshop to help you develop your active listening skills.

### Exercise

In threes, one person is the coach, one the learner and one the observer. The learner needs to speak for two minutes on what the challenges are for him/her currently in his/her present role. The coach needs to listen with the intention of understanding but saying nothing. The observer needs to note down what is happening in terms of the behaviour of both the coach and the learner. At the end the observer needs to give feedback to the pair, finding out the following.

- Did the learner feel listened to?
- What was the coach actually doing to make the learner feel listened to?
- How did the learner feel?
- What was the effect on the learner of the coach not saying anything?
- What was the effect on the coach of not saying anything?
- For the coach what was getting in the way of listening?

The purpose of this activity is to highlight to the coach what is helping and what is getting in the way of listening for learning. Once we strip away the need for the coach to be thinking of what question to ask next, what actually happens? Does the coach's inner dialogue come into play? Is the coach more or less able to focus on what the learner is saying when he/she is silent? What are the key non-verbal signals to someone that actually convey to him/her that he/she is being listened to?

COACHING FOR SCHOOLS

After mastering the skills of active listening the next stage in listening for learning is responding.

If we are listening to understand, there are going to be times that we need to check out with the learner that we understand what is being said. It can be a struggle to try and concentrate on every word that's being said by the learner and there is such a thing as trying too hard. It is best to try and concentrate on the main themes of what is being said and regularly check understanding with the learner. By summarising what the learner is saying, the coach will be both moving the learner forward and clarifying the coach's understanding at the same time.

*Summarising and reflecting back*

When summarising, the coach will be using phrases like:

- 'As I understand it what you are saying is . . .'
- 'From what I am hearing, you are telling me . . .'
- 'So am I right in thinking . . .'

As these phrases are checking and verifying what has been said, they need to be offered in a slightly tentative way. By using a tentative approach and maybe offering half a comment, the coach can be sure that he/she is not putting words into the learner's mouth. The coach has to be careful that, in summarising and paraphrasing what the learner is saying, he/she does not put his/her own 'spin' on the learner's story.

The following example shows how easy it is to put your own interpretation on what someone else is saying.

## Coaching conversation

Sharon – a secondary school year head – has come to see James, her line manager, for a debrief, for which he is using a coaching style, following an unsuccessful internal job interview.

JAMES: So Sharon, how do you feel about yesterday?

SHARON: Disappointed and let down really.

JAMES: Tell me more about it.

> SHARON: Well I put so much work into the presentation. I spent all weekend on it and I feel it was all for nothing. I felt that I had thought of everything in the presentation and it was just a waste of time. I should have spent more time preparing for the questions.
>
> JAMES: So what I am hearing you saying is that the presentation went really badly.
>
> SHARON: No, I was told that the presentation was the best part of my interview; all I am saying is that I spent too long on it. Why, have you heard any different from anyone?

What James should have said was:

'So, just to check out my understanding, you felt that the time spent on your presentation was at the expense of preparing for the questions.'

This would have simply reflected back what Sharon was already thinking. Instead she immediately got worried and defensive, thinking that James had heard that her presentation did not go well.

Reflecting back to the learner purely what you think they have said eliminates any possibility of the coach interpreting the information that is coming from the learner.

### KEY POINT

**Coaching is not about interpreting the information that you hear, it is about being 100 per cent focused on the learner and his/her agenda.**

Listening is about the coach leaving the detective work at home because, if the coach is trying too hard to interpret the information the learner is presenting, then he/she will not be listening effectively. All the coach's energy will be focused on framing the next question and using his/her own reference points to interpret the information rather than trying to arrive at a deep understanding of the learner's issue.

COACHING FOR SCHOOLS

The following is an example of the coach using too much interpretation.

> ### Coaching conversation
>
> Jason is a new head of science and is having a coaching session with his line manager, Mary, an assistant headteacher, who is using coaching to develop Jason's leadership skills.
>
> MARY: So tell me Jason, how do you find your new role?
>
> JASON: It's going quite well. I am just about getting my head around it. There's so much to do: prioritising and time management are difficult and it's hard to think about what is the most important task to do when it all sounds urgent. I scarcely have time to turn around. I just don't have the time that I used to have to spend on my own planning and teaching. I have always prided myself on being an excellent practitioner and I sometimes wonder if that can still be my priority.
>
> MARY: So Jason, what I am hearing you saying is that you are afraid that your own credibility as an excellent science teacher will be damaged by your lack of time for planning and your credibility as head of department will be diminished as a result.

At which point did Jason say that he was worried about his credibility as head of department? That was Mary's interpretation, she read too much into what Jason said and her response probably worried him further. Jason's concern was merely one of how to prioritise the demands of his new role and a more useful response would have been:

Mary: So what I am hearing you say is that you are finding it difficult to give the same time to your teaching and planning while fitting in the new tasks as head of department.

Here Mary successfully reflects back the facts of what Jason said.

*Suspending judgement*

Another important aspect of listening for learning is being non-judgemental. While listening, it is very easy for the coach to give off signals to the learner of approval or agreement, prompting the learner to want to please the coach. If the coach gives his/her own value judgements on the learner's actions or thoughts then the coaching session begins to centre on the coach and what he/she thinks rather than the learner. It is important that the coach remains in a neutral state

THE ESSENTIAL SKILLS OF COACHING

so that he/she can hold a mirror up to the learner, reflecting back the learner's agenda. When it comes to the learner committing to actions it is essential that his/her choices are not influenced by what the coach thinks. Conversely, it is important for the coach not to show disapproval of what the learner is telling him/her. There is nothing more likely to close the learner down than a coach's perceived disproval. This is a particularly important feature of listening when the coach is in a higher managerial position to the learner. In a coaching session it is important that the learner goes beyond wanting to please the coach and telling him/her what he/she perceives he/she wants to hear. Progress with issues can only happen if there is an open and honest relationship between coach and learner. The coach must outwardly show that he/she is approaching the session with a non-judgemental attitude.

The following example illustrates this point.

### Coaching conversation

Karen is Peter's headteacher. They are having their regular monthly coaching session. Peter is teaching a particularly difficult Year 5 class and is feeling the stress of next year's Standard Assessment Tasks (SATs).

KAREN: So Peter, tell me what sort of a half term has it been?

PETER: Dreadful, I have felt really at the end of my tether and I know you will not be very happy about the way I have organised the curriculum this term, but it is a case of having to, I'm afraid. I have to consider the children I have got in my class and what their needs are. I know it does not fit in with your way of seeing things but I am the one on the ground and I need to respond to my class and their needs.

KAREN: So tell me more about the needs of your class.

PETER: Well they don't even know the basics and I have got several with behavioural difficulties and what they need is a strict programme of revision coming up to SATs with every minute of their day organised and timetabled so that there is no room for disruptive behaviour. Plenty of pen and pencil work and not much movement around the class. I know this goes against what we decided in the excellence and enjoyment INSET day but I feel it's what the kids need.

KAREN: So what I am hearing you saying is that the class do not know the basics. What do you think the best way for them to learn is?

Karen avoided passing her own judgements on the way in which Peter had approached the difficulties that his class presented. This was difficult for her as the school had already established that it was going to follow a more creative style of curriculum. Peter was obviously not following this. She managed to resist the temptation to criticise Peter and chastise him for not adhering to school policy. At that time, as she was coaching, she was trying to reflect back to Peter what he perceived the needs of the class were and hopefully he would arrive at his own more individual solution to the problem.

*Empathy*

When listening for learning, showing empathy to the learner is a key feature of good communication and rapport-building.

Empathy and sympathy can be confused. When holding a coaching session the learner does not want the coach's sympathy as this will get in the way of progress. If the coach relates what the learner is saying to his/her own experience and expresses sympathy, then the coach is not using that third level of listening that is required. The coach needs to remain slightly detached from what the learner is saying. Sympathy would come into that second level of listening – directed listening. In directed listening the coach is making an effort to understand the learner by relating his/her own life history to the learner, seeing what he/she has in common with the learner and expressing sympathy. A sympathetic listener will respond to the learner by saying things like: 'How terrible . . . I know what you are going through . . . You really were treated badly . . . I am so sorry . . . I know just how you feel'.

Empathy is a skill of a higher order than sympathy; empathy is trying to understand the learner's reality as he/she sees it. It will give the coach accurate information to deal with because the information will be free from the coach's interpretation. So often when we are listening to someone we will be solution-focused. Instead of trying to hear what the other person is saying we will be coming up with ideas from our own experience, which we think will help them. In order to help someone you need to take time to understand how *he/she* sees things. This is showing empathy. Providing a quick-fix solution to a problem that can be followed in three easy steps is an easy and rapid way of problem solving. However, this approach will encourage dependency on the part of the learner and could frustrate and anger him/her.

## Coaching conversation

Lucy is approaching her colleague Ken, who had previously taught her year group, for some advice and the following conversation took place.

LUCY: I was thinking about how to group the class, as I don't think the current groups are working. Maybe they need to be different for the core subjects.

KEN: I know just what you mean; I had exactly the same problem. I have got my old groups on the laptop. Come along after school and I will give them to you.

LUCY: No that's not it. Anyway we have had two new kids in since last year and they have changed the dynamic. I just wondered what you thought about having different groups – what the pitfalls were.

KEN: Just follow my groups from last year, it won't cause you any problems – they are used to them. They worked for me.

Lucy would have come away from this conversation angry and with a feeling of not being listened to. What she wanted was to have a discussion with an experienced colleague on the merits of grouping for different subjects. Instead all she was offered was a quick-fix solution. There was no attempt to understand her or what she was saying. Worse still, Ken assumed that what worked for him will work for her.

Ken demonstrated a non-empathetic approach to listening, in that he focused on what he thought he heard. An empathetic approach to listening will focus on what is actually being said rather than what the person thinks is being said.

## KEY POINT

**In coaching, the learner is coming up with his/her own solutions, which have been arrived at by his/her own deep learning, facilitated by the coach. An empathetic listener will hold back from offering his/her own answers, so that deep learning on behalf of the learner can take place.**

People with good levels of emotional intelligence (EI) will be able to show empathy with the learner and have a commitment to developing his/her true potential. They will also be able to control their own emotions, which is important when a coach is trying to be non-judgemental and have a high degree of objectivity at all times. People with high EI also show a high level of optimism, which is very important, as coaching is all about moving forward and building a better future with your staff.

| Coaching building blocks | | |
| --- | --- | --- |
| Rapport-building | Listening for learning | Effective questioning |

## Effective questioning

### Different types of questions

As teachers we are used to asking children questions. We ask questions for many reasons. There are different questions that are designed to perform different functions. We will ask questions for the following reasons.

- **To clarify our own understanding** 'As I understand it, then, are we changing the playground duty rota so that there are always three adults out there at any one time?'
- **To see if the learner remembers/understands** 'Who can tell me how a flower is pollinated?'
- **To seek information** 'What is the recommended adult–pupil ratio for school trips?'
- **To gain agreement** 'Does everyone agree that we are going ahead with this?'
- **To interrogate** 'Why did you not do your homework?'
- **To find out someone's opinion** 'What do you think of the new style of school dinners?'

These questions are at quite a superficial level and do not require much thinking on the part of the learner. In coaching we are concerned with asking questions at a deeper level. A good coach – like the good teacher – will ask questions that get the learner to think for him-/herself. For most of the questions a coach asks there will be no right answer.

We occasionally hear teachers actually say, 'That was not quite the answer I was looking for'. In coaching we must give up looking for the right answers. Our function as coaches is to ask challenging and powerful questions that unlock issues for our learners.

# THE ESSENTIAL SKILLS OF COACHING

> **KEY POINT**
>
> Being questioned is something that can challenge and clarify your own thinking in a way that moves you forward. If you are asked a powerful question, in formulating your response you will often be thinking of the issue in a completely different way.

You often hear yourself answering a question, thinking 'I have never thought of this before'. Those key moments of learning, when it is as if someone has turned a light on, often occur as a result of answering a powerful question.

The ability to ask searching and challenging questions is essential for a coach. Coaching is not a cosy chat and in order for the client to move forward the client does need to be stretched. A school that is planning to use coaching sessions will have to establish at the outset how challenging it is prepared to be when asking questions. Asking challenging questions can seem threatening at first. However, in a coaching session, getting someone out of his/her comfort zone can be very rewarding in the end. How far a person is prepared to be challenged will need to be negotiated. If you challenge someone too much they will just close down and all the potential for learning will be lost. The level of challenge someone is prepared to take is different for each person and the coach needs to be sensitive to this.

## Exercise

In pairs, make a list of the most powerful questions that you have ever been asked. Compare them with your partner's to see if there are any common elements. Make a note of the ones that really made you think and begin to build a bank of powerful questions. Here are some to start you off.

1. What would you do if you could not fail?
2. What would you do if time, and money were no object?
3. What could you do to make this fun?
4. What is the best possible outcome?
5. What is the worst that can happen?

A coaching question needs to be:

- open
- challenging
- visionary
- exploratory
- powerful

## COACHING FOR SCHOOLS

### *Open questions*

An open question is one which there is no right answer. The answer is not going to be yes or no. The question is going to be framed in such a way that the learner's responses are going to be far longer than the coach's questions. Don't forget that, in a coaching situation the learner is supposed to be doing 70 per cent of the talking and the coach 30 per cent. Closed questions encourage the learner to be lazy and get away with doing very little thinking and exploring.

An open question will interest and stimulate the learner. The learner may present the coach with an either/or situation for which the only question appropriate seems closed. For example:

*Learner: There are a number of things to be done at the moment; I am running out of time for writing the end of year reports.*

> **Coaching conversation**
>
> A closed question would be:
>
> MANAGER: Will they be completed by the deadline?
>
> The answer to this is either 'yes' or 'no' and requires very little thinking from the learner. It also provides the manager with the problem of what to do about it. The learner has placed the problem at the manager's feet. The learner has raised the problem and now the manager has to find a solution.
>
> An open question would be:
>
> MANAGER: When could they be ready by?
>
> LEARNER: Well I could get them done by Monday, but I will need someone to cover for me on Friday afternoon... I could ask Sandra.

By asking an open question the manager has prompted the learner to think through his own solution to the problem.

### *Challenging questions*

A question that challenges the learner will lead him/her to make progress and uncover layers of his/her issue or situation that are below the surface. A challenging question may unblock barriers that are impeding his/her progress. In answering a challenging question, a learner will develop a greater awareness of

THE ESSENTIAL SKILLS OF COACHING

the issue and build a different perspective. In asking a challenging question you may be delving into some very entrenched and deeply held beliefs by the learner. That is why the coach has to use his/her sensitivity and tread carefully if needed.

The following is a situation described by a new member of staff to her manager during a coaching session.

### Coaching conversation

LEARNER: I am feeling really uncomfortable going out on the playground after school. None of the parents will talk to me. It's always the same, wherever I go, I can't seem to make an impression with the parents, they just ignore me. I think it's because I am young – I just don't look like a teacher.

MANAGER: So none of the parents ever talks to you?

LEARNER: Well, no, actually some of them do.

MANAGER: Which ones?

LEARNER: Mrs C and Mr G, usually to tell me reasons why Kieran has not done his homework and to check on his behaviour.

MANAGER: So Mrs C and Mr G do talk to you?

LEARNER: Well yes some of them do, but not many on the playground, not like they do to the other staff.

Here we see the coach challenging the statement 'None of the parents speaks to me'. The coach did it in a subtle way, reflecting back the learner's language at the same time. The coach could have said something like 'that's ridiculous, in the six weeks you have been here surely SOMEONE must have spoken to you'. Instead the coach gently challenged the statement provoking the learner to think about it.

### Exercise

Read again what the learner said in that example. There are some beliefs the learner has that could be holding her back. What are they and what challenging questions would you ask to unblock them?

45

*Challenging questions to shift limiting beliefs*

Coaching is about unlocking someone's potential. As a coach it is important that you believe in a person's power to change and develop. In a coaching session, say, on doing some data analysis, you may hear someone say something like 'I can't to that, I never have been able to . . . I am not a numbers sort of person'.

People give themselves labels from very early on in life. You often hear it of someone who has a bad experience, say, with sport at school. From then on they will label themselves and say things like 'I am not a sporty person'.

> **KEY POINT**
>
> People put limits around themselves about what they can and can't do, but these are self-imposed limits not absolutes.

With challenging questions a coach can challenge lifelong held beliefs that may be limiting people.

Have a look at the following example.

### Coaching conversation

The head is doing the annual interview with each teacher to establish who will teach which year group in the following year. Susan has always taught Key Stage 3 and has become rather stale. Also, there are other members of staff whom the head would like to move into Key Stage 3. The head would like to develop Susan, who is a good teacher.

HEAD: Now as you know I am very keen on moving people around so how do you feel about taking another year group next year?

SUSAN: I am a Key Stage 3 teacher, that's what I trained as, that's what I am good at.

HEAD: So you see yourself as a Key Stage 3 teacher?

SUSAN: Yes I do. I have done so for the past ten years and that's where I feel comfortable.

HEAD: What would have to happen to make you feel comfortable in another Key Stage?

# THE ESSENTIAL SKILLS OF COACHING

This is a skilful question because it does not contradict Susan's limiting belief. Instead it cleverly puts teaching in another Key Stage as a possibility without actually saying that. It takes a proactive attitude to the situation rather than dwelling on the negative aspect.

### *Visionary questions*

Visionary questions are literally questions that prompt the learner to see what he/she is talking about, perhaps with new eyes. If you are asked a visionary question you will be asked to use your imagination and picture what you are thinking about. When you are asked to put into words what you can see, you suddenly clarify for yourself what it is you are aspiring to. These questions are particularly useful at the goal-setting stage of the coaching process.

For instance, in the following example, Jane is carrying out a performance management interview with Carol, who is head of modern foreign languages. They are trying to set a goal concerning leadership.

*Jane: I want to improve my subject leadership skills. I want to get better at leading the department. I can't really describe it, but I know I don't do it very well at the moment. I don't want to be running around in circles like I am now. I want to be a highly efficient department leader. Yes, that's my goal.*

*Carol: What does a highly effective department head look like?*

This visionary question will make Carol unpick what it is to be a good department head and then pin her down to which aspect of the role she wishes to frame the goal around. You could also word this question for the auditory communicator: 'What do you hear an effective head of department say and what would staff be saying about you?' Or the kinaesthetic communicator: 'What does it feel like to be led by an effective head of department?'

Other visionary questions could be:

- 'Imagine you are at your own retirement party, what do you see, what do you hear people saying?'
- 'When you see yourself in five years' time, what do you see yourself doing?'
- 'Imagine your perfect working day, where are you, what are you doing? What does it look like?'

A good visionary question that can move a whole school forward when development planning could be:

- 'What will this school look like in ten years' time?'

## COACHING FOR SCHOOLS

*Exploratory questions*

These are questions that are going to encourage the learner to be more reflective and explore the topic. They, may be given to the learner as homework and encourage him/her to understand him/herself and his/her job more thoroughly. They could be used in performance management interviews to identify strengths and areas for development.

Examples of these are:

- 'What are you putting up with at the moment?'
- 'What motivates you?'
- 'What does it mean to be a good leader/team member?'
- 'What does it mean to be successful in your job?'

Exploratory questions will also clarify the situation for both the coach and the learner. They can sometimes be offered to the learner in a tentative way, even a half-formed question using the learner's language may provoke the learner into some deep reflective thinking.

### Coaching conversation

LEARNER: I have been struggling with my role as a line manager of the lunchtime supervisors. They are quite an opinionated group and I always seem to get into a confrontational situation with them at meetings. They just don't seem to see the need to change anything. The merest suggestions of making any improvements to lunchtimes and they just go off at a tangent, saying that everything is OK and it is the children who are getting more difficult.

COACH: They go off at tangents... tell me more about...

LEARNER: More about what they actually do go on about? Well, they bring up the same old chestnut of not having enough staff out there; they say if they had another person in the team they could manage all the lunchtime disputes.

The coach tentatively offered a question. The learner latched on to it and finished it for him.

Through a half-suggested question, the coach has uncovered what the real issue is for the lunchtime supervisors.

*Powerful questions*

Powerful questions can move the learner on light years. They can really get to what the hub of a problem is and are best used when the learner seems at a dead end or if it seems that the real issue is being disguised. They are short and cannot be avoided. They will demand an honest and truthful answer. Powerful questions will go beneath the surface and probe what the learner knows already and uncover endless possibilities.

## Coaching conversation

LEARNER: I just can't get started writing the new scheme of work. I am not going to meet the deadline. There seems no point writing it now as everything is going to change anyway, due to new guidance coming out soon from the LA. The other reason is we have three new members of staff joining us in September, so there does not seem much point in starting it now without their input.

COACH: So what do you want to happen?

This question puts the issue very much back in the learner's domain of influence. Never mind all the outside influences, what does the learner actually want to see happening?

Other powerful questions are:

- 'What is the truth here?'
- 'How will you know?'
- 'How can you tell?'
- 'What's stopping you?'
- 'How will pupils benefit from this?'

An important skill a coach needs in relating to questioning is the ability to frame questions in a positive and open way, designed to illicit full and illuminating answers. A learner may be approaching a topic in a very negative way and it is the coach's job to reframe the topic using questioning.

For instance, the learner may come up with the following scenario.

*Learner: There is no way that I can give my student the time she wants. She is asking to meet me every day after school for a post-mortem on her teaching for an hour. I just can't do it. I should never have agreed to have a student. I did not realise it would be this much work. I just can't do it justice, it really is not working.*

*Coach: OK, so you can't meet every day for an hour, what could you do?*

The coach immediately puts the responsibility on to the learner to come up with a solution to the problem and turn it into a positive, solution-focused discussion.

### Chapter summary

In order to be a successful coach, you need to practise the skills of:

- rapport-building;
- effective questioning;
- listening for learning.

If you build rapport then the learner will feel at ease and relaxed. You can demonstrate that you have a rapport with someone by mirroring a person's language and non-verbal signals.

In a coaching session you need to ask effective open-ended questions. Your questions will be aimed at gaining a better understanding of where the learner is. Your questions will need to challenge the learner.

When coaching, make sure that you listen to learn. Listen at a deep level in order to understand and show empathy with the learner. Remember that the coach is talking 70 per cent of the time and the coach 30 per cent.

## Your learning in practice

### Exercise

1. What elements of the building blocks of coaching are you already good at?
2. How do you know?

## THE ESSENTIAL SKILLS OF COACHING

You may find the following format useful in deciding this.

| The building blocks of coaching that I am already good at | Evidence/examples |
|---|---|
| Rapport-building
*Specific elements:* | |
| Listening for learning
*Specific elements:* | |
| Effective questioning
*Specific elements:* | |

Skim read the chapter headings and list any skills you may not be as good at or have less experience in.

Use the template below to identify your development areas.

| Building blocks | Specific area for development |
|---|---|
| Effective questioning | |
| Rapport-building | |
| Listening for learning | |

3. Think of the ways in which you can develop and practise your skills. How will you know when they are achieved?

| Development area | Activity identified to practise/develop it | Evidence that it has improved |
|---|---|---|
|  |  |  |

## Learning review

What do you need to do now, in terms of further reading, discussing with staff and trying ideas out, to embed that learning?

Plan what you are going to do within the next month and put aside a time to do it.

| Coaching development plan |||
|---|---|---|
| Reading | Discussing with staff | Experimenting |
| What? When? |  |  |
|  |  |  |
|  |  |  |

# 3

# The coaching process

## This chapter in short

This chapter will provide you with a coaching model to use in your coaching sessions. The coaching model will provide a structure for you to build your coaching sessions around. The model will cover what to do in a coaching session. The chapter will show you how to use the model, how it can be adapted and you will be able to go away and plan your coaching sessions.

## Objectives

By the end of this chapter you will be able to:

- be clear about what has to be agreed before a series of coaching sessions needs to take place;
- understand the need for a model;
- be able to move through the different stages of the model;
- identify useful questions for each stage of the model;
- think of some practical suggestions for making the model work;
- use the model to plan your coaching sessions.

## Before you start

Before the actual coaching sessions take place, there are protocols and details to be worked out to enable both the coach and the learner to be clear about the process and what to expect.

If you are going to embark on a coaching programme with the whole staff, this initial meeting can be done through a staff meeting with everyone present. If you are coaching a colleague independently you will have to have a context-setting meeting during which you and your colleague make clear expectations of each other and the way in which you are going to proceed.

The roles and responsibilities of both the coach and the learner will be established in this session. Time spent in this session agreeing these will set the scene for the learner/coach relationship. There may be pressure from the learner in this session to start talking about the issues or coaching topic, but the coach must resist this.

Both parties in this first session need to clarify what the other one wants to achieve. During this session the coach needs to make clear to the learner that the coach believes in the learner's capacity to improve his/her performance in whatever field it is that he/she is covering. The coach must make it explicit to the learner that he/she is confident that the learner has the potential to be developed. It is in this session that the rapport talked about in Chapter 2 needs to be established.

## The pre-coaching meeting

The client should be made to feel valued and understood during this crucial first session. The coach will be using the skill of *listening for learning* to really establish the context of the coaching sessions.

It may be useful to have the learner fill in some information sheets before the first session and possibly even read a description of what the mutual expectations of the coach and learner are (for examples see the coaching arrangements table on page 57). The pre-coaching meeting needs to establish the following:

## THE COACHING PROCESS

### When and where the meetings will take place

This will need to be somewhere quiet and comfortable where there are no interruptions. In some schools finding somewhere like this will pose a problem. If you do meet in someone's office it is important to ensure that someone else will answer the phone and deal with knocks at the door.

### Frequency and timings of sessions

How often you are going to meet and for how long needs to be established. An average coaching session will last an hour, but it is a very intense activity for both the coach and the learner and sometimes 45 minutes is enough. It is the coach's responsibility to be the timekeeper for the sessions. The gaps between sessions can vary but a month is a useful period of time, which gives the learner some time to take action without losing focus.

In terms of how many sessions are needed then this will vary but it needs to be agreed at the outset. Some coaching topics will need a single session. For instance, a team leader may decide to coach a member of his/her team who is about to give a presentation. This will need one session only. On the other hand, a school that is introducing a new initiative may decide that staff need to be coaching each other once a month for the whole academic year. My suggestion is that when you start coaching you take on a small short assignment and build on that.

### How to make time for the sessions

This is perhaps the most crucial element to get right. If arrangements are not made that detail how time is freed up for the coaching sessions to take place, then they will not happen. If coaching is to become embedded in your school then you have to plan for how staff are going to be free to carry out the work. Some schools have successfully built this into their meeting times, scheduling them at the beginning of the year.

### What work is to be done in between sessions?

Right from the outset it needs to be made clear to the learner that he/she will be expected to carry out some work in between sessions. This may not need to be very onerous, in fact it may only be some thinking on the part of the learner. It is important to gain agreement to this because it forms part of the learner taking responsibility for his/her own growth and development.

### Expectations of the coach and learner

The learner needs to be confident that he/she can say anything to the coach and it will be treated with respect and confidentiality. Anything that the learner shares with the coach, be it of a personal or professional nature, needs to be treated with absolute confidentiality. The coach also has a right to be treated with respect and this will mean that the learner must keep appointments and be punctual.

It is useful to clarify expectations of both the learner and the coach. The following is a suggested list of expectations which the learner and coach can agree to.

*As your coach you can expect from me:*

- total support and commitment to your goals;
- confidentiality;
- belief in your potential for growth and development;
- I will listen to you without passing judgement on what you say.

*As a learner you can expect from me:*

- punctuality and a commitment to work together;
- I will undertake any agreed actions in between sessions;
- I will understand that I am responsible for creating my own results;
- honesty and openness during coaching sessions.

### Responsibility for note-taking

During a coaching session much will be spoken about and agreed. The learner may leave the session wanting some record of this to reflect on and refer to in between sessions. The coach and the learner need to decide who is responsible for taking notes during the session and what the function of the notes will be. If the learner takes notes, then he/she will only take note of the most pertinent parts of the discussion for him/her, which could be part of his/her learning. Expecting the learner to take notes will also mean that he/she is taking responsibility. However, you may decide that it is better for the coach to take notes because that frees up the learner to talk and explore issues unhindered. Note-taking needs to come at the end of a session when what has been discussed is being summarised, so that the flow of conversation during the session is unimpeded. (See the following table for note-taking formats.)

My suggestion is that the coach and learner, at the beginning of each group of coaching sessions, fill in a coaching arrangements sheet to finalise the above points (see the following table).

THE COACHING PROCESS

---

**Coaching arrangements**
Name of learner:
Name of coach:
Date:

---

Broad area of coaching, i.e. subject leadership, thinking skills

---

Time and place of meetings

---

Period in between meetings

---

Session length

---

Note-taking arrangements

---

Period of coaching assignment

---

Coaching explanation and expectations agreed
Yes, No            Date:

Any other comments

---

# The first session

In your first session you will be clarifying the protocols above and deciding on how to work together. It is important from the outset to establish what in the long term the learner is expecting to get out of being coached and what the purpose is. Although the purpose of the coaching session may have been decided in a staff meeting beforehand, one person's understanding of an issue will be very different from another's. No one person's reality is the same as another's and we all bring our unique understanding of the world to coaching.

> ### Case study
>
> Name of school: Three Fields
>
> Context: Inner-city primary
>
> Three Fields School, in inner-city Nottingham, had decided to invest in coaching and all staff had had training in coaching skills, which had been very well received. The trainer/coach had been contracted to do a one-day skills workshop for the teaching staff to be followed up with four skills development sessions. It had been decided by the head and the trainer/coach that the focus of the coaching in school would be subject leadership and the teaching staff were split up into pairs to coach each other on aspects of this role. Before the trainer/coach came into the school again it was agreed that each coaching pair would have had two coaching sessions on an aspect of their subject leader role. The focus of the first skills development session would be on finding out what the issues were in their coaching pairs and further embedding of the coaching model.
>
> When the trainer/coach went into the school for this first skills development session, she found that none of the coaching paired sessions had taken place. The trainer/coach was faced with the task of somehow moving forward.
>
> The trainer/coach then carried out coaching sessions with each pair to try and find out what had gone wrong and try to renew their commitment to coaching. On talking to the teachers it emerged that the subject leadership was a huge issue in school and a few of the staff were unclear about what it entailed. They could not coach each other on subject leadership when they were unsure about what it was. There was no agreement in school about what was expected of a subject leader. There was no breakdown of the role and what the specifics of the role were.
>
> The teachers felt that they could not make a start because they were unclear about what the purpose of the coaching sessions was.

In this instance the trainer/coach had to get back to basics. What was immobilising the teachers was the enormity of the task and a lack of knowledge of the area in question. They were new to the concept of coaching and struggling to take it on as a concept and were unfamiliar with the territory on which the coaching sessions were based. No wonder the coaching had not happened!

Lessons learned:

- be explicit with the staff on why the coaching training is taking place;
- be clear about what the purpose of the staff learning coaching skills is;
- involve staff in the decision to adopt a coaching approach;
- when staff are coaching for the first time, make it a very narrow focus;
- to begin with, make the topics staff coach each other on something non-threatening that they are already familiar with;
- when staff move on to coach each other on whole-school issues, make sure that there is a consensus on what those issues are.

### Scope of the sessions

As well as being clear about the purpose of the session both the coach and the learner need to establish, in the first session, the area that the coaching assignment will cover. If coaching is linked to a whole-school initiative then that may be clear. However, even if the whole school teaching staff is working on, say, subject leadership, the area of focus may be different for each teacher. For instance, one member of staff may need to look at his/her subject knowledge and another may need to explore using data. The coach will also need to establish what sort of context the learner is working in. In a small school this may appear obvious, but in a larger school the coach will need to know what size the department is and details like the staff's level of competence. The coach will also need to establish what the learner's expertise in this area is already. The learner will not be approaching the coaching sessions like a blank book, and highlighting strengths and weaknesses will give the learner a good lead into goal-setting. All of this preliminary work will feed into the first session on goal-setting in order for it to be very focused.

In conclusion, the first session needs to cover:

- the purpose of the coaching assignment;
- the topic and scope of the coaching sessions;
- the context in which the learner is working;
- what the learner sees as his/her strengths and weaknesses already in this area.

You have had your preliminary meeting, your protocols are agreed, you are both clear on the purposes of the coaching assignment. You are ready to begin using the coaching model.

## Why a model?

> **KEY POINT**
>
> Coaching is a conversation but it is not a cosy chat. One of the elements that formalises it is the structure, i.e. the model of the conversation.

A model for your sessions will provide a framework for your coaching conversations.

Much of coaching is intuitive and you probably have informal coaching conversations all the time in school. However, a proper coaching session needs an established structure so that both the coach and the learner know where they are going. There is nothing wrong with an informal coaching conversation in the staffroom or in the corridor; in fact these can be illuminating. The problem with them is that both the coach and the learner can come away from them without a clear idea on what has been agreed. Who is going to decide when and where the next session is and what the agreed action will be? We have all been in the situation with someone who just catches you for a word or two on the way to a meeting and you end up in a coaching-style conversation. The trouble with that is you realise you have had a similar conversation with that person over the same issue months ago and no progress seems to have been made. The same old issues keep coming up. This is because if you have the same old-style conversations not really leading anywhere, you will end up with the same recurring results. A dedicated coaching session built around an agreed structure will move the learner forward in a way that the informal conversation will not.

A model for your sessions will add rigour and pace to your coaching conversations. After all, the school will have made an investment in coaching in terms of time and training, so a system of coaching that makes good use of time is appropriate.

# THE COACHING PROCESS

The model we will be looking at has four distinct phases and you will be able to plan your coaching sessions around these.

## What is coaching?

Coaching is a series of structured conversations in which the coach supports the learner in developing aspects of his/her role in school. The goals that the coach and learner will be working on will be decided by the learner around the area of his/her job, which has been agreed beforehand.

As a learner in a coaching situation you will be asked questions by the coach that sometimes challenge you. Much of the impact of the coaching session will happen afterwards when you begin to reflect on what was said during the session and the effect that it has had on your thinking.

Your coach will listen to you, question you and reflect back to you what you have said to enable you to gain a better understanding of your situation and how to move forward.

Coaching is not counselling or therapy and if issues are touched on during the coaching sessions that are more appropriate to a counseling session the coach will bring the session back to its coaching purpose.

Coaching relies on the learner taking responsibility for his/her own development and total ownership of his/her own growth. The learner therefore will not be looking to the coach for the answers to the issues that he/she brings to the session.

Although there is a structure for the coaching sessions that we will be following, it is not a one size fits all formula. There may be times when stages of the model need revisiting and different stages may need to be looked at out of sequence. As you become more practised as a coach you may find that your coaching sessions become more intuitive and have a natural flow to them. However, you will still need a system for revising your progress with the learner and a pathway for the learner to follow.

Intuitively following the flow of a coaching conversation is fine for the more experienced coach, but for those still finding their way the model is a useful tool to follow.

## The four stages of the model

As coaching will initiate a leap forward in the development of the learner I have called our coaching model **LEAP**. It has four stages:

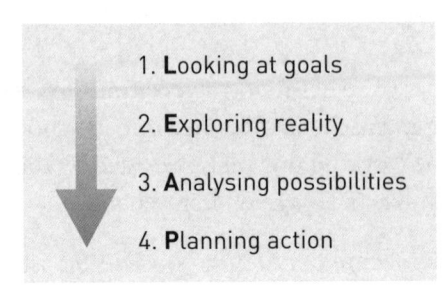

1. **L**ooking at goals
2. **E**xploring reality
3. **A**nalysing possibilities
4. **P**lanning action

In general the four stages of the model should be followed in order. The stages will take varying degrees of time. For instance the session on stage two *Exploring reality* may only take one session. Whereas, *Looking at goals* may take two sessions. What may also happen is that halfway through a series of sessions you may find that the learner's goal has changed and he/she needs to revisit *Looking at goals* again. This is fine as long as you keep the model and its stages at the back of your mind as a coach and eventually follow them. The other thing that may happen is that the context of the learner may change if he/she has moved schools or roles within a school and you may need another session on context-building.

Now let's look at each stage in more detail.

## Stage one – *Looking at goals*

### Why set goals?

We have all set goals. Probably every January we set a goal appertaining to losing weight and getting fit, or to read more, or spend more time with the children. Most probably these goals are not achieved and forgotten about by February and that is because they were good intentions rather than a goal. A learner will need to work with a coach to raise his/her aspirations above the level of a good intention to a clearly defined goal.

Goal-setting is a powerful tool, which can be used as a way of moving people from where they are to where they want to be. If you don't set a goal how can you measure how far you have come and indeed if you have arrived? You will have seen in school how goals are set every year and written into the school improvement plan. Everyone will share in the sense of achievement and excitement when these goals are fulfilled. Setting a goal as an individual will give you confidence and a sense of achievement and move you forward to achieve more than you ever thought possible.

The benefits of setting goals include:

- increased confidence because you can measure your growth;
- better self-esteem when you have met your goals;
- encouraging you to become more proactive about your own development;
- it provides you with focus and direction.

## The nature of the goal

With goal-setting it is vital to the process that the learner has ownership of the goal. If goals are imposed there is little chance that they will be achieved or, if they are achieved, the learner will not gain the learning and growth from the journey of achieving them that he/she should have done. It is not only the actual achievement of the goal that is important but, more significantly, the learning, growth and development that goes on throughout the journey. If the learner's goals are related to those of the school the learner will need to rephrase them so that it makes sense to him-/herself and his/her situation.

For instance, if a school goal was: *To achieve average or better value added scores in Key Stage 2 maths SATs*, the learners would have to think about what part they could play in achieving that whole-school goal. If they were maths subject leaders, their goal may be: *To fulfil the strategic planning aspect of the subject leader role.*

Part of that role would involve an action plan to move the maths in the school forward to achieve the school goal.

Goals need to be specific enough so that they can be measured; it is helpful here to use the SMART acronym to help formulate your goal:

- Specific;
- Measurable;
- Attainable;
- Realistic;
- Timeframed.

Although goals do need to be attainable there does need to be a good level of challenge. It is important that goals should stretch the individual out of their comfort zone. The coach will be able to judge how much challenge and stretching is appropriate.

Although measurability is important when forming goals, it is vital that goals are not just restricted to topics, which can be easily measured. Goals related to pupil attainment are easy to measure, but what about softer goals? For instance: *to increase pupil independence when learning.* The task of measuring that goal could be very interesting indeed and finding a way of doing that would involve the learner in defining what exactly an independent learner looks like. Rather than restrict goal-setting to easily quantifiable subjects, a skilled coach will encourage the learner to find ways of assessing those more difficult goals. This process will lead to a better understanding of the goal itself.

A coaching discussion around *Looking at goals* would begin with a wide discussion on the topic. The coach would help the learner move from broader aims to actual goals. This stage of the process is set in the future. The learner is thinking of what he/she wants to achieve. You may sense that the learner is getting a little nervous and trying to limit the goal to what is obviously easily achievable. This could be because he/she fears failure. It is important at this stage that the coach reassures the learner that goals can be reworked and revised at any stage of the coaching process. In fact revisiting goals and checking out if they need revision should be part of every coaching assignment.

The rapport and trust built by the coach will come in here and he/she will be able to judge whether the learner needs challenging or he/she will need a series of relatively achievable goals to achieve at first in order to build confidence. A key aspect of forming goals is the words we choose. Many people will have a tendency to word goals as things they want to stop doing. For instance: *to stop raising my voice in the classroom.* If the goal stays as it is the learner will focus on what he/she must not do. Instead it needs to be reworded into positive active language. For instance: *to use positive behaviour management strategies in the classroom.* You can see straight away how the learner is going to focus through his/her goal and begin to build a constructive agenda for change.

In order to enable the learners to be in the right frame of mind for goal-setting, you can try some visioning with them.

The following is a suggestion for how to encourage the learner to actually see what success looks like.

### Visioning your goals

A coach says, 'Imagine that you are at a time and place in the future when your goal is achieved. Take some time to take yourself forward to that time when everything to do with your goals is as it should be. What is happening? What are people saying to you? How are you feeling? What are you seeing that tells you you have achieved your goal?' In this example the learner will be able to make his/her goals real: actually see them.

Depending on your rapport with the learner and his/her learning style, you may try asking the learner to draw a picture of what it looks like to achieve his/her goal. The reasoning behind this is that he/she gets to know what an achieved goal looks like. If the learner has in his/her mind's eye an idea of what, say, effective behaviour management looks like, then he/she will be able to recognise it when it happens.

### Effective questions in *Looking at goals*

Here are some questions to help you with this stage of the coaching model.

- What is it you actually want?
- When specifically do you want it?
- What will it look like when it happens?
- How will you know when you have got there?
- In which situations do you want to achieve this goal?
- Who will it affect?
- How will things be different when you have achieved it?

### Winding up the *Looking at goals* stage

It is important at the end of this session to check out the learner's commitment to the goal that he/she has formed. Some carefully worded questions will establish the level of enthusiasm and ownership a learner will have regarding the goal.

- How real is this goal to you?
- If you could have it right now, would you take it?
- How much influence do you have over this issue?
- What is getting in the way of you having this?

COACHING FOR SCHOOLS

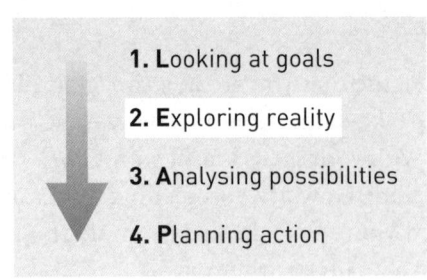

1. **L**ooking at goals

2. **E**xploring reality

3. **A**nalysing possibilities

4. **P**lanning action

## Stage two – *Exploring reality*

Having established the learner's goal, in other words where they want to be, you now need to establish where he/she is. The skill of the coach at this stage is to get the learner to be analytical and objective when describing the current situation. This stage of the model is very firmly set in the present. In the *Looking at goals* stage the coach was encouraging the learner to be creative and visionary. In *Exploring reality* the coach is making sure the learner is rooted in reality, in other words – what is really happening.

The coach will need to employ his/her *listening for learning* skills and try to understand exactly what the situation is. The aim of the session is to gain a clear picture of the issue as the learner sees it.

The coach should remain as objective as possible at this stage and avoid using evaluative or emotive language. The main focus of the session should be on the facts. The coach will have to pin the learner down to be as detailed and specific as possible about the situation. During this session the learner will be encouraged by the coach to tell his/her story. It will be at this time that the real issues are clarified.

It may seem that this stage of the model should come first so that the coach can get an idea of what the situation is before the goals are set. However, the reason why goals are set at the beginning of the process is that it provides a clear direction for the conversation to follow. It is important that goals are set first, however loosely, and they may need redefining after the *Exploring reality* stage.

### KEY POINT

As a coach you will be raising the awareness of the learner to his/her situation and encouraging him/her to take responsibility.

The following is an example.

## Coaching conversation

Steve is a deputy head in a large, leafy suburb comprehensive school. A member of staff, who has been appointed lead coach in the school on management and leadership issues, is holding a coaching session with him at this second stage – Exploring reality.

COACH: So Steve, we have established that your goal is to manage your time more effectively. Tell me, what's happening right now that tells you there is a problem with this?

STEVE: I am missing deadlines and I am not happy with the quality of my work.

COACH: Can you be more specific?

STEVE: Yes, last week I was asked by the assessment coordinator to collect all the reports from all the year heads and go through them before parents' evening and I forgot to ask for them, which meant running around at the last minute, chasing people. It didn't look very good.

COACH: How often does that type of thing happen?

STEVE: It feels like all the time.

COACH: All the time?

STEVE: Well, maybe once a fortnight at least. I seem to have left something to the last minute and be rushing around. It does not look good; I am supposed to be setting an example.

COACH: What sort of example?

STEVE: I should be the first one to meet deadlines and be acting in an efficient and organised way.

COACH: So you want to be seen as efficient and organised?

STEVE: Not only seen to be, but that's how I want to be for myself. I am feeling pretty bad about my ability to do the job at the moment.

COACH: Which part of the job makes you feel like that?

STEVE: I suppose the bit that has me running around like a headless chicken and missing deadlines.

COACHING FOR SCHOOLS

> COACH: Do you miss all deadlines?
>
> STEVE: Mmm... no, sometimes they seem easier to meet.
>
> COACH: Which deadlines seem to present the problem?
>
> STEVE: The ones that involve other people... the ones that mean I have to ask people to do things. That's what I have a problem with.
>
> COACH: So let's look again at what actually is the problem here.
>
> STEVE: I suppose it is the bit that involves holding people accountable. I put off asking them to do things because I know how busy they are and I feel bad putting them under more pressure.
>
> COACH: So what is it that's stopping you being more efficient and organised at the moment?
>
> STEVE: Well it is... well one of the things is this reluctance to ask people to do things.
>
> COACH: Is that something that we could work on?
>
> STEVE: Yes.

You can see from this conversation how the coach followed Steve's interest and let him establish the direction of the conversation. By the coach focusing on the situation, as Steve saw it, they were able to uncover the real issue. The coach would go on to define a goal concerning accountability. At no time did the coach try to bring Steve back to the previously set goal on time management. Instead, the coach has followed Steve's train of thought and given him the confidence to uncover the real issue. The coach developed Steve's awareness of the problem and brought Steve to a realisation of what the actual nub of the problem was.

Effective questions at this stage include:

- 'What is going on at the moment in this area?'
- 'What is actually happening?'
- 'How often does it happen?'
- 'How does that make you feel?'
- 'What have you done so far to improve things?'
- 'What is getting in the way that prevents you from moving forwards?'

# THE COACHING PROCESS

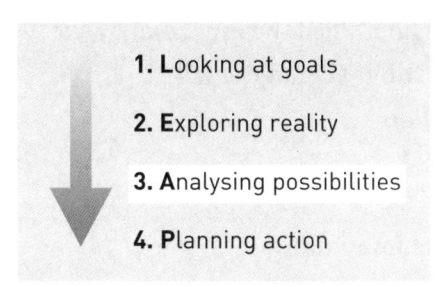

1. **L**ooking at goals
2. **E**xploring reality
3. **A**nalysing possibilities
4. **P**lanning action

## Stage three – *Analysing possibilities*

The focus of this stage is on possibilities, not answers. The skill of the coach lies in enabling the learner to unleash his/her imagination to discover all sorts of ways that the set goal could be achieved, no matter how far-fetched or unattainable it may seem. There is no point at all in setting the learner's sights, at this stage, on what is easily attainable. The learner's goal may seem unrealistic, but it is important not to close down the learner's thinking by restricting it to only thinking of what is possible. We have left reality behind in the last stage and we are now focused firmly in the future again, with blue-sky thinking.

The skill of the coach lies in opening up the learner's thinking so that he/she can be as creative as possible. Whether suggestions for meeting the goal are possible or not is immaterial at this stage. It is from this wide selection of creative ideas that the learner will choose a selection of action points.

Through thinking creatively and widely, at first some obstacles that are seeming to get in the way of the goal being achieved will sometimes disappear. You discover what the real barriers are and what the imaginary ones are.

If the coach does not encourage the learner to think as widely as possible from the beginning of this session then the choice of actions to select from for the action-planning process will be too narrow. The process of creating this list of options is as important as the result. The coach has to create an atmosphere in which the learner feels uninhibited and free to suggest anything at all.

The coach will have to draw on his/her skills of being non-judgemental. It is vital that the learner does not pick up any signs of disapproval at any suggestion that he/she makes.

The statements below best illustrate this process of thinking broadly and gradually narrowing down ideas that the learner may be making at this stage:

- 'What the ideal solution would be'
- 'What I would like to do but it is impossible'

- 'What I could do if I had the time, money, etc.'
- 'What I would do if I could not fail'
- 'What I might do'
- 'What I will do'

## Restrictions – real or imagined

You can see straight away how restricting it would have been to start with 'What I will do'. That would immediately put limitations on what was possible. Obviously, there are restrictions of time, money and resources that affect anything that goes on in a school, but, to begin with, it is important to free up the learner and let him/her think creatively without hindrances. Sometimes lack of resources can be used as a reason not to move forward. For example:

*Mark was a maths subject leader in a large primary school. The headteacher had explained at the beginning of the year that the budget was extremely tight and there was nothing left for curriculum development. There were no subject budgets that year. The staff had undergone some training by the lead maths teacher on calculation, which was on the School Improvement Plan as a priority. The calculation methods shown to the staff involved the use of number lines. Two months after the training in her regular termly meeting with him, the headteacher asked Mark how the new methods were working out. Mark replied that they had not been introduced because there were no number lines and under her instructions about curriculum spending he had not bought any. Clearly the headteacher could have found some money for number lines. Had Mark used the lack of resources as a real or imagined reason not to implement the new methods?*

You often hear people say 'We would like to do this but . . .' Take away the 'but' for a while and just be free to think about what is desirable and then work out how this can be resourced.

> **KEY POINT**
>
> Some limitations that people put on themselves are real, others are imagined.

This is best illustrated by an exercise I use in training sessions. It is used as an icebreaker with training on teamwork.

Delegates are divided into teams on the day. Each team has to make the tallest structure they can using 10 jelly babies and 20 sticks of spaghetti. There all always disputes about the team who wins, usually over the issue of cheating! Some people think that the winning team has cheated others think that they have thought creatively. Some teams imagine that there are restrictions on the exercise, but who said that the jelly babies could not be cut in half? Who said that it was against the rules to stand the structure on a pile of books? In fact there are no rules just a simple instruction. The team that has thought most creatively around the task usually wins. The teams that lose have put limitations and restrictions on the task that are not really there.

> **KEY POINT**
>
> **What coaching can do is explore all possibilities and work on the barriers that are preventing progress.**

It is important that all ideas and possibilities are recorded at this stage as the coach is going to lead the learner to look at all of them.

The coach and the learner need to look together at each option and weigh up its strengths and weaknesses. It is important also for the coach to test out the commitment of the learner to each option on a scale of one to ten.

The following is an example of the coach encouraging the learner to think around a limitation.

## Coaching conversation

Julia, a newly appointed head of a small rural primary school in Somerset, is working on a goal of raising the profile of her school, which has had a history of poor leadership and erratic SAT results. The recent Ofsted inspection labelled the school as 'improving'. The school is desperate to increase numbers in order to survive.

COACH: So Julia, what are the possible things you could do to raise the school's profile?

JULIA: Well we have done a lot already. I can't really think of anything else.

COACH: OK, what if you could think of something else?

JULIA: I could invite the local press in, but to be honest they gave us such a hammering over the Ofsted the chair of governors has vowed never to

COACHING FOR SCHOOLS

> speak to them again. She has warned me against having them in school.
>
> COACH: Just suppose for a moment that there was no problem with the press. What could you do?
>
> JULIA: Well, we have got an open day coming up. I could invite them.
>
> COACH: Good, what else could you do?
>
> JULIA: The previous head went around all the playgroups with the school brochure, I could try that again. Actually, I could invite them to the open day... in fact I could have a separate open day for the pre-school parents and their children and publicise that at the nursery.
>
> COACH: Anything else?
>
> JULIA: Not really, the governors say they have tried everything else.
>
> COACH: I have got a few ideas do you want me to offer them to you?
>
> JULIA: Yes please.
>
> COACH: You have a village fête coming up, why don't some of the children dress up and do the maypole dancing that you did in the spring.
>
> JULIA: That's great and I could get the PTA to do a cake stall and maybe we could do an exhibition of the artwork from Arts week.

You will observe that the coach offered the learner a suggestion. Clearly if the coach has expertise in the area that the learner is generating ideas on then it would be permissible to offer those ideas. The crucial word here is *offer*. The coach needs to ask the learner if he/she would like some suggestions that should be regarded simply as one of the many on a list of options.

The other interesting thing is that having been released from the restriction of not inviting the press in, the ideas flowed. The coach would have revisited the issue of the chair of governors and the press and examined if that was a real or imagined barrier. Maybe the Chair had moved on in her thinking since the Ofsted report and the bad press the school had received.

Effective questions for the *Analysing possibilities* stage include:

- 'What would you do if failure was not an option?'
- 'What would you do if you had all the time and money in the world?'
- 'If you secretly knew what to do, what would you do?'

THE COACHING PROCESS

- 'What would you advise a friend or colleague to do?'
- 'What else would you do?'
- 'If you knew the answer, what would you do?'
- 'Looking at all of these options, choose the one that is going to move you forward just one step. Choose the easiest one that you feel most comfortable with and start with that. How will this one thing move you forward?'

Write down what the benefit of this one thing will be.

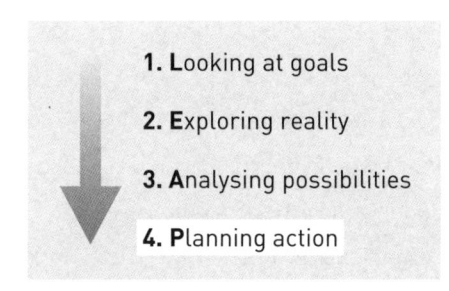

1. **L**ooking at goals

2. **E**xploring reality

3. **A**nalysing possibilities

4. **P**lanning action

## Stage four – *Planning action*

This is the 'doing' stage of the model. School staff will be used to making action plans so this is the stage that they will probably feel most comfortable with.

During this stage you will be working with the list of options you have generated and selecting the most appropriate to start with and planning what the next steps will be. This stage is set in the future. However, it is important to agree what is to be done now so it is set in the immediate future.

The coach will take quite a tough line of questioning here and pin the learner down to say what he/she will actually do. It is a good time to check out the learner's commitment to the agreed actions. The coach will have changed the emphasis from what could happen to what will happen. The coach will encourage the learner to be action-focused and think of the possible barriers that might prevent action from being taken and how to deal with them. The coach can check out the learner's commitment by the tone of his/her voice and body language. Questions will centre on the what, when and how of the actions agreed. There is a degree of accountability at this juncture and the learner needs to know how these actions will be followed up. In an organisation like a school it would be nice to think that all staff are self-motivated and do not need any follow-up. Human nature being what it is, the coach may need to establish with the learner when the follow-up coaching session will take place, so that there is an aim.

COACHING FOR SCHOOLS

## Coaching conversation

Tom, an NQT, is having a coaching session with his mentor about the goal of cutting down on the time he devotes to marking children's work. Tom has come up with a list of options and it is now time to plan his next steps.

COACH: Now, out of all the options we discussed last time to cut down on marking, which ones appealed most to you?

TOM: I am not sure I remember them, what do you think?

COACH: Well let's look at the list and go through them. We have got the following:

- marking a focus group at a time;
- getting the children to self-mark their own tests;
- setting open-ended investigations as homework;
- doing more investigations in class and just marking them at the end of the unit;
- altering your routine so that three days a week after school you spend the first half-hour marking, rather than going to the staffroom.

Which one of those do you feel most comfortable with?

TOM: The last one. I have actually started to do that already and it has made a big difference. I now go to the staffroom when I have done some marking and I need a break.

COACH: Good, so you have made a start. What else are you going to do?

TOM: The one about the focus group.

COACH: When are you going to start that?

TOM: I suppose after the half-term holiday would be good.

COACH: OK, how committed on a scale of one to ten are you to introducing that after half-term?

TOM: Err... Seven... maybe.

COACH: What is stopping it from being a ten?

TOM: Well I can see it would be of benefit but I am not sure how it actually works in practice and how the kids would respond.

COACH: So you need some support on this. Who could help you?

# THE COACHING PROCESS

> TOM: Well, Jim the deputy is doing it, maybe he could help.
>
> COACH: So, with the help of Jim, what is the number now?
>
> TOM: It has gone up to a nine but not a ten because I am still not quite sure.
>
> COACH: Nine is fine. When are you going to ask for Jim's help?
>
> TOM: By the end of the week.

The coach has asked a direct question that is crucial at this stage, 'How committed are you on a scale of one to ten to carrying out this action?' Anything less than an eight means that the learner is not committed enough to carry out the action. The question 'What would it take to make it an eight?' identifies potential barriers and obstacles. One of these obstacles for Tom was that he needed support. It is a good idea, during planning for action, to identify the support needed and also who else may need to know or be involved in this action.

When we are coaching someone we are coaching for success. All too often in our work we have 'to do' lists that never seem to be complete and grow longer every day. This leads to a sense of dissatisfaction and can lower self-esteem.

By establishing the commitment of the learner, the support needed and the possible obstacles, we are building in success for the learner, that's why it is important to start with the thing that they feel most comfortable with.

Effective questions at this stage include:

- 'What are you going to do?'
- 'When will you do it?'
- 'Does anyone else need to know?'
- 'When will you tell them?'
- 'What support will you need?'
- 'How and when will you get it?'
- 'What may be stopping you from carrying out this action?'
- 'On a scale of one to ten, how committed are you to taking this action?'

The form the action will take will vary from person to person. However, the basics of what will happen, when it will happen and how it will happen do need to be covered. For those who like a little more detail, the following are some suggested formats for action planning at the end of this chapter.

# COACHING FOR SCHOOLS

## Formats for recording sessions

| Name:<br>Email:<br>Phone number:<br>Current role:<br>School:<br>Date: |
|---|
| Goals |
| List of options |
| Resources/support needed |
| Barriers/challenges |
| Agreed action with timescale |

THE COACHING PROCESS

Name:
Email:
Phone number:
Current role:
School:
Date:

What are your goals?

How will you know that you have achieved them?

What will you do to achieve them?

When will you achieve them by?

Who will support you in achieving them?

| Name: |
| Email: |
| Phone number: |
| Current role: |
| School: |
| Date: |

| Goals |
| --- |
|  |

| Actions – when are you going to take them? |
| --- |
|  |

| How will these actions meet your goals? |
| --- |
|  |

| What are the obstacles involved? |
| --- |
|  |

| To what extent are these obstacles real or imagined and, proportionally, how much are they created by you, how much by others? |
| --- |
|  |

THE COACHING PROCESS

> **Chapter summary**
>
> In order for a series of coaching conversations to achieve results they will need to follow a structure. The LEAP model provides a framework for your sessions. Different questions are appropriate to different stages of the model. Each coaching session will cover a stage or stages of the model. Stages can be revisited and revised, particularly that for goal-setting.
>
> Pre-coaching meetings need to take place before a coaching assignment can begin.

# Your learning in practice

### Exercise

1. What stages of the LEAP model do you think you are going to find the easiest?
2. Which stages are you going to find trickier?

You may find the following format useful in deciding this.

| Elements of the model that I find easy | Elements that I am going to struggle with |
|---|---|
| Looking at goals<br>*Specific elements:* | Looking at goals<br>*Specific elements:* |
| Exploring reality<br>*Specific elements:* | Exploring reality<br>*Specific elements:* |
| Analysing possibilities<br>*Specific elements:* | Analysing possibilities<br>*Specific elements:* |
| Planning for action<br>*Specific elements:* | Planning for action<br>*Specific elements:* |

What are you going to do to about those problem areas?

- Read more?
- Discuss with a colleague?
- Have a go at a coaching session with a learning partner?
- Reflect on what you do already that may be similar and you may be able to build on?

# How to develop a coaching culture in your school

## This chapter in short

This chapter will give you the essential ingredients for starting a programme of coaching in your school. It will examine the common pitfalls that can happen when introducing coaching and discuss how to avoid them. It will provide a model for successfully embedding coaching in the school's culture.

## Objectives

When you have completed this chapter you will be able to:

- look at dealing with barriers to coaching;
- examine the issues of the leader as coach;
- show how your school can become a learning organisation;
- provide a framework for introducing coaching into the school.

## Introducing coaching – laying the foundations

Introducing coaching into the school will represent a substantial investment of time and money. It is therefore vital to the success of the project that all staff are involved from the outset. There is no one way of introducing coaching to the school. You may be working in a school where the senior leadership team or just the headteacher is receiving some coaching. There may be a few members of staff with some knowledge of coaching. On the other hand you may be in a school where the only knowledge of coaching is the fact that you are reading this book.

Whatever the starting point of the school one thing is clear. In order for the initiative to work, staff have to be clear about what the purpose is. It is advisable to start the initiative with a training day for all staff. This will dispel any misconceptions of coaching among the staff. It could be that a move towards coaching may be viewed with suspicion by staff and this could impede its impact. Some training in the principles of coaching for all staff will ensure that coaching can be high on the school's agenda. The other purpose of the training day is for the school to develop a shared definition of what they mean by 'coaching'. No one will come without any knowledge at all of coaching. Some staff may have read books or articles in magazines about 'life-coaching'. Others may have had some experience of coaching through the Key Stage 3 strategy. People in the school may be experienced mentors. Working on a shared definition will confirm what coaching is in the context of the school. If this is cleared up at the outset then introducing coaching will be more likely to succeed.

One of the first things to be done when starting a training day on coaching with the whole staff is to establish what they know already about coaching. The day then moves on to actually defining what coaching is. One of the first things staff need to know on a coaching training day is why they are doing it and what the purpose is.

### KEY POINT

**All staff need to know what the long-term goals are of introducing coaching to the school. They need to know why they are attending an INSET day and what is in it for them.**

The outcomes of introducing coaching need to be agreed, made clear and shared with all staff before any training can take place. Some of the reasons for introducing coaching are to:

- make the performance management cycle more meaningful;
- embed new strategies;
- establish a learning community among the staff;
- build on successful mentoring experience;
- encourage staff to learn from each other;
- have less reliance on consultants;
- support collaborative leadership;
- enhance and embed any INSET;
- improve the skills of subject leaders;
- support pupils with barriers to learning;
- raise standards in the quality of teaching and learning.

The reasons are many and varied. The important thing for a school is to work out how coaching is going to benefit it. In other words, why are they doing it?

## Who is going to be a coach?

Having worked out the purpose, the next step is to sort out how it is going to be used. Who is going to coach whom needs to be established and what the topic is needs to be agreed. Which groups of staff will be trained and who will do the coaching needs to be discussed. It may be that the head has decided to introduce coaching to the whole staff as a valuable tool for their work. When they will be expected to coach and who they will be coaching needs to be established. There are various groups of staff that can use coaching skills with other staff and pupils. Some examples are:

- performance management leaders with their teams at review meetings;
- pupils who act as peer mediators with pupils;
- teaching assistants who are acting as learning mentors;
- senior leadership team coaching each other on leadership issues;
- subject leaders being coached by the senior leadership team;
- teachers who are doing peer coaching on a particular teaching and learning strategy;
- teachers who are working with the school's council as a way of resolving issues.

## Building success into coaching

To be really successful, coaching needs to be a part of the school improvement plan with clear goals and allocated time and resources. Otherwise it will be hijacked by developments that emerge during the year. The most successful work done has been when the head has already seen the benefits of coaching and had a successful experience of coaching first hand.

> **KEY POINT**
>
> If the headteacher, or team leader, is enthusiastic and supportive of coaching, he/she will drive the whole thing forward and make it happen.

The head or a senior member of staff needs to be clear about the benefits of coaching and what it has done for them in order for them to be able to sell it to the staff.

The leadership team of the school needs to support the introduction of coaching into the school. Otherwise it will fail.

Coaching is not a short-term strategy and needs time to embed and make a difference. That is why I would recommend a model that introduces coaching over a school year. It is not enough to spend a day teaching the staff coaching skills and then expect it to just happen. There needs to be a structure of coaching workshops throughout the year, whereby the trainer can lead sessions on skills development. The other activity that can be built in is for members of staff to be coached during the year on the progress of their coaching. The coach would then be modelling the skills as a way of embedding the learning.

How to build success into introducing coaching:

- secure the commitment of the head or senior leadership team;
- make clear to staff the purpose and focus on the desired outcomes;
- ensure that it is on the SIP;
- involve all staff in the training;
- work out a shared definition of coaching.

## Working out a strategy to introduce coaching skills

When writing an action plan on how to introduce coaching into your school, it is useful to treat it like a coaching session. Some of the headings from the LEAP model are useful here. For instance, *Exploring goals* will lead you to think of what it is you want the project to actually achieve for your school.

Let's look at two very different case studies and see how this was done.

### Case study

Name of school: Freshfields Primary/Nursery

Context: 300 pupils on roll, inner-city setting

Freshfields had been through a period of four years without a substantive headteacher. There had been a succession of acting heads and the governors had advertised and failed to appoint a headteacher three times. The previous headteacher had ended his career at the school and retired due to ill health. Prior to his retirement he had been on long-term absence due to sickness. The result was that Ofsted judged the school to have serious weaknesses and the staff had lost confidence. Freshfields seemed to be the school that just could not move forward.

The LA had put a range of support measures into the school but there seemed to be an implementation gap. The staff would go on training and get very enthusiastic and then they would come back to school and nothing would happen. The LA teacher/coach had worked with staff and they were positive about her work.

The school was a member of the Education Action Zone, which had meant it was involved in various behaviour and curriculum developments. However, no matter what training and support the school had, the attainment was getting worse and the standards of teaching and learning remained only satisfactory.

The LA decided to put in a county headteacher for two years to try and turn the school around. The new headteacher felt sorry for the staff and felt they had been the 'Cinderellas' of the local area. She felt their professional development had been neglected. She wanted them to learn coaching skills as a way of giving them back their confidence. What was particularly poor in the school was subject leadership. The head hoped that coaching would move people forward in their subject leadership roles.

The headteacher was only going to be at the school for two years and saw herself as a troubleshooter for the county. She had a very 'pace-setting' style and was conscious that there would be an Ofsted inspection soon.

COACHING FOR SCHOOLS

The Education Action Zone offered the headteacher a consultant/trainer to work on introducing coaching skills to the staff at no cost to the school.

The headteacher and consultant came up with the following action plan.

### Goals

To establish a sustainable leadership team with the coaching skills to lead the school forward

### Strengths

Strong headteacher with clear agenda for improvement
Members of an Education Action Zone
Effective deputy head with wide range of experience

### Barriers/challenges

Some negative staff attitudes
Lack of continuity of headship
Lack of leadership experience from the staff
Staff feel wounded, lack of staff confidence

### Agreed action

1. Train and embed coaching skills in staff
2. Practise and monitor coaching skill development
3. Coach leadership team on roles
4. Coach subject leaders on roles
5. Empower staff to perform their leadership role using coaching model
6. Evaluate effectiveness of training

---

During the coaching training day, the headteacher introduced the trainer but then did not attend. The staff were very receptive to the training and wanted to try out the new skills. Towards the end of the day the trainer asked if there were any questions. One teacher asked 'Why are we doing this?' It became apparent that the staff did not even know prior to the training day what it was going to be about. They certainly seemed to have no idea about what they were doing or why.

The trainer tried to explain what the goal of using coaching in their school was, although it would have been better coming from the headteacher. The training was very well received with the verdict from one member of staff ▶

being 'This is the best ever INSET we have had'. All looked very promising for a good start to coaching in the school.

The head and trainer had produced the following programme of training to embed the skills within the school:

| Term 1 | | | Term 2 | |
|---|---|---|---|---|
| INSET day | Coaching twilight to review progress | Coaching twilight on subject leadership | Leadership team coaching | Coaching twilight to review progress |
| | Term 3 | | | Term 4 |
| Coaching twilight further coaching skills development | Leadership team coaching | Coaching twilight on subject leadership | Leadership team coaching | Evaluation |

It was decided that the best way to embed the coaching skills into the school was a combination of the leadership team being coached themselves and further skills development for the whole staff.

At the end of the training day staff formed coaching pairs and set up their first coaching sessions with a time, a place and an issue. The following month the consultant arrived at the school to find that everything had not gone as planned. The coaching pairs had fallen apart – reasons being that 'It's too emotional, it makes me cry'. Coaching sessions had not taken place. The staff were under enormous pressure as they being observed by the LA and there had not been time allowed for coaching.

---

**What went wrong?**

Coaching was not high enough on the agenda at Freshfields. This was made evident by the headteacher not attending the training day. The teachers had no idea as to what the purpose of using and learning coaching skills was. There was no common understanding developed beforehand of the principles of coaching. Perhaps most importantly coaching was being used as a remedial measure to shore up the leadership at subject leader level.

COACHING FOR SCHOOLS

> **KEY POINT**
>
> Coaching will not work as a remedial measure on its own. It will obviously improve things but it is not a quick sticking plaster that will make the situation better instantly.

**What should have happened at Freshfields?**

Any INSET is doomed to failure unless staff attending know what to expect. The other elements they need to be involved in are the purpose of the INSET activity and where it will lead. Most people will sit in on an INSET day and think 'what's in it for me?' People need to be reassured that time has been put aside for them to use the skills they have acquired.

The headteacher should have shown to the staff that she had a greater commitment to the coaching training. Her non-attendance at the INSET day made the staff suspicious. This was accentuated by her own pace-setting style.

Let us now look at our second case study.

> **Case study**
>
> Name of school: Naildon Comprehensive
>
> Context: 1200 pupils, suburban setting
>
> Naildon school had a good reputation locally but the headteacher and the governors felt it was coasting. It was the type of school that served a small suburban town and there was no other choice for students that did not involve getting on a bus and going out of town. The head was worried that the pupils had a passive attitude to learning. In an area of high employment with good living conditions the students did not have very high aspirations. They were confident of getting a job no matter what their grades were. The head also felt that discipline at the school was not of a high enough standard. Too much lesson time was lost after lunchtime on sorting out playground disputes. The students needed to develop more of a sense of responsibility for themselves and their environment. Because it was a middle-class school the staff seemed to feel that there were no discipline problems. The number of exclusions and serious incidents was low. As a result, much low-level disruption and rudeness was tolerated in the classroom and this slipped over to the lunchtimes. ▶

## HOW TO DEVELOP A COACHING CULTURE IN YOUR SCHOOL

The deputy headteacher had alerted the head to the fact that it was some years since the performance management (PM) team leaders had undergone introduction of coaching skills as a way of bringing a fresh approach to the PM interview. It would also make the team leaders take a more proactive approach to their role.

The headteacher had had some executive coaching on leadership issues that he had found very valuable and was very interested in using coaching in its wider sense. The deputy head had seen the benefits of coaching through the Key Stage 3 strategy.

The senior leadership team had discussed the idea of introducing peer mediators into their initial training and some were new to the role. The deputy saw the learning mentors in school. The peer mediators would be students who had been trained in coaching and mediation skills, supervised by lunchtime staff who had also been trained. The learning mentors would be teaching assistants who would be using coaching skills to unblock the students' barriers to learning.

What was emerging was the need to train staff in coaching skills. The other agenda was that the senior leadership team hoped that coaching would make the staff and students more proactive and revitalise their passion for learning.

The senior leadership team worked with the trainer/consultant to agree the following action plan.

### Goals

To establish a coaching culture within the school

### Purpose of coaching

To reinforce the school as a learning community
To improve the PM cycle
To help with student discipline
To develop a skilled workforce with a shared vocabulary
To enhance leadership skills

### Applications

For PM team leaders to use in reviews
For peer mediators to use skills at lunchtimes
For learning mentors to use in supporting students with barriers to learning
For teachers to use in peer coaching on improving discipline
For the leadership team to use at meetings

COACHING FOR SCHOOLS

**Agreed action**

- Share agreed outcomes with staff
- Develop a clear but flexible action plan
- Make it a strand of the SIP
- Make a member of staff the lead coach who will receive coaching sessions
- Hold regular review meetings with the trainer/consultant

By the time the coaching training day had taken place there had been four meetings with the senior leadership team. In these meetings there had been a common understanding established of what was meant by coaching and the purposes of the project were clearly defined. Due to the high numbers of staff, they were trained in separate teams. The head introduced the trainer to the teams at each training session and explained what the purposes and expected outcomes of the training were. A member of the senior leadership team attended all the training events.

The training events were embedded with the following actions.

| Term 1 | | | Term 2 | |
| --- | --- | --- | --- | --- |
| Four meetings with the senior leadership team to establish context of school and agree outcomes for project | Regular coaching sessions for head and senior team | Consultant to write action plan using coaching framework with SLT | Training events for all teams | Follow-up training with learning mentors |
| | Term 3 | | | Term 4 |
| Review meeting with deputy head | Further skills workshop with PM team leaders | Review meeting with deputy head | Training of peer mediators | Evaluation of first year |

**What went well?**

The project at Naildon is still in its early stages but the signs are that it is going well. Whenever the consultant arrives at the school she is expected and staff are eager to share their coaching experiences with her. The deputy head reports that he has noticed staff being less passive and coming to him suggesting initiatives. There is more talk about teaching and learning in the staffroom with staff being eager to share expertise and ideas.

The round of PM interviews has gone very well with staff feeling that they have more ownership of the process. They also feel that their targets have been more relevant. The number of incidents at lunchtime is dropping. One knock-on effect that no one expected is that staff actually feel more cared for. Coaching and life coaching have been very much in the media with their benefits for personal development being stressed. As a result of having learned coaching skills staff feel more able to develop their own potential and those of others. The reason they feel cared for is that the school has seen fit to invest in them by teaching them those life skills.

The section of the training that covered listening skills was very well received by staff. Listening for meaning rather than telling is a strategy they are trying to use with the students.

Having learned the skills of listening for meaning there is a common understanding between staff on what it means to listen and there are far fewer misunderstandings between them. Staff have also reported that the listening for meaning skills have also benefited their dealings with parents and conflict resolution with students.

## Why did it go well at Naildon?

- The head and deputy had already had positive experiences of coaching.
- There was time invested in planning and agreeing outcomes built into the action plan.
- The strategy had the full backing of the headteacher who was enthusiastic and keen to establish a coaching culture within the school.
- The senior leadership team had already established a common definition of coaching.
- The senior leadership already had an idea of how coaching could be used.
- All staff understood the big picture of why coaching was being introduced.
- Each staff team was clear about what part it should play in the strategy.

## Embedding success into coaching

Reflecting on both of these case studies it is easy to see why one failed and the other one succeeded. How you introduce coaching into your school will depend

COACHING FOR SCHOOLS

on your circumstances and context. You may start a pilot project with a group of staff. You may find that, having done NCSL's 'Leading from the middle', your middle leaders want to become coaches themselves. Whatever way you decide to do it the purposes and the expected outcomes need to be established beforehand rather than doing it just because it sounds like a good thing to do. Instead of introducing coaching to all staff you might decide that the best way to start is to do some coaching yourself. You have read this book, you have done the exercises, you are now ready to practise on someone. Perhaps you are a team leader and have some responsibility for managing the team. Maybe you are a teacher who would like to pair up with someone else and just use coaching as a way of learning on the job. You could also be a consultant who would like to use these new skills with your schools.

## Practising coaching

The one thing you need when developing coaching skills is to practise. A good way of doing this is to find two other like-minded colleagues. You could form a coaching trio. In your coaching trios you can practise coaching with one person being the coach, one the observer and one the learner. The idea is that you have three sessions in which the roles are rotated.

The role of the observer is to keep a record of behaviours and questions that the coach asks and what the coach does. It is useful for the observer to keep a record of this.

### Coaching triads observation sheet

| Skill/attribute | Notes and examples |
|---|---|
| 1. Builds rapport | |
| 2. Demonstrates active listening | |
| 3. Chooses open-ended questions | |
| Looking at goals, supports learner to: <br> ■ set priorities; <br> ■ identity clear outcomes; <br> ■ focus on most important issues. | |

92

Exploring reality, supports learner to:

- explore the current situation;
- identify limiting beliefs;
- recognise strengths.

Analysing possiblities, encourages learner to:

- consider a range of options;
- think outside the box;
- think creatively.

Planning for action, helps learner to:

- decide which option will meet the goal;
- draw up an action plan;
- agree timescales;
- commit to taking action.

Each coaching session needs to be short – about 15 minutes. Then the observer needs to have a chance to give feedback for five minutes. The learner also needs a chance to report on how it felt and what he/she found useful. Make sure that you choose an appropriate issue to be coached on.

### How to pick an issue

It must be . . .

- current and unresolved;
- something you want to do something about;
- not necessarily a problem, could be an opportunity;
- not necessarily something small, could be the whole thing.

This whole process will take 25 minutes, which, if it is done once a week, hardly presents much of a time commitment. Every three weeks one person gets the chance to be a learner, which gives a chance for some action to be taken in between.

This model of learning works really well and the benefits are that all three members of the triad are learning from each other and being coached at the same time. Whether you are doing this as one group of three in your school or doing it with all staff, the effect is that it leads to good collaboration between staff. Clearly, choosing the triads is important. You need to find people with whom you feel comfortable and who you trust. You need to agree on ground rules such as confidentiality. It is a good idea to choose two other people who are not doing exactly the same job as you in school. This offers some distance and objectivity.

The best way of getting started in these triads is to choose an issue to be coached on that is small. The area of coaching when you are starting needs to be something that is not that important. Just getting started is the crucial thing and it is vital that people don't get bogged down and intimidated by the responsibility of dealing with a huge issue. Ideas for low-key issues to begin with are:

- cutting down on marking;
- giving a presentation;
- talking to parents;
- improving plenaries;
- prioritising tasks.

Once you have had about six practice sessions in your triads you will be ready to do some coaching yourself.

## Session planning

If you feel that you have had enough practice and are ready to start a coaching assignment with someone, you need to have a plan. A coaching plan model I suggest consists of 8 sessions of about 45 minutes. These sessions will be spaced over the year with about three-week intervals in between them.

| Session 1 | Session 2 | Session 3 | Session 4 | Session 5 | Session 6 | Session 7 | Session 8 |
| --- | --- | --- | --- | --- | --- | --- | --- |
| Establishing the context of the learner | Goal-setting | Ongoing coaching using LEAP model | Ongoing coaching using LEAP model | Review progress | Ongoing coaching using LEAP model | Ongoing coaching using LEAP model | Evaluation |

Now you are ready to get started it would be wise to look at some of the pitfalls that can beset coaching. There are some barriers that can stop coaching working effectively. If we examine them here then at least you will be prepared for them and can deal with them if they arise.

# Coaching – what can go wrong

Let's look at the most common barriers that can stop coaching succeeding.

1. *Environmental problems*

   When you are coaching someone you need to be in a place that is conducive to the activity. In a school that may be difficult, but as the coach it is your responsibility to provide such a space. It is important that the room is well ventilated, with water provided for both the coach and learner. The seating needs to be arranged so that the coach and learner are comfortable without getting too sleepy!

   The room needs to afford the right amount of privacy for the learner to feel relaxed about what he/she is saying. There needs to be enough quiet so that both the coach and learner can hear each other without too much effort.

   If the coaching environment is not right, then coaching can get off to a bad start, which is difficult to recover from.

2. *The time factor*

   Lack of time is a common cause of coaching not succeeding. We have already spoken about the importance of maintaining a firm commitment to coaching. Anything in a school that is being introduced needs time allocated to it. If there are coaching sessions planned then clearly these cannot be expected to be in staff's own time. Obviously the most efficient way of scheduling time for coaching sessions is to organise release time. If this is not possible then the most common way to free up time is for a team or staff meeting to be devoted to coaching once a month.

   When you are deciding when coaching sessions are going to happen, make a firm commitment that they will not be cancelled. Time is also an issue within a coaching session. We have already established that 45 minutes to an hour is the optimum time. However, I have had very productive sessions from between 15 minutes and 2 hours. It is up to the coach to manage the time effectively for each session. For the learner, you do not want him/her to feel hurried. On the other hand, you do not want him/her to mention what the real issue is in the last few minutes and not have time to be able to discuss it.

   One way around this is to be very up front about how the time is going during a session. It is useful to say things such as 'We have 20 minutes left, what would you like to cover in that time?' After a while the coach will develop the skill of creating a relaxed climate while managing the time efficiently.

   Being a coach is a hugely rewarding experience but it is hard work and can be draining. In order to maintain as much concentration as possible, the coach needs to build in breaks between coaching sessions of 15 minutes each. There is also a limit to how many coaching sessions you can fit into one day. If you are working as a consultant, working in a school on coaching assignment, you need to give consideration to your coaching timetable.

3. *People problems*

   Not everyone will want to be coached and the coach can find him-/herself coaching difficult people. Some people may find coaching questions intimidating and threatening. Coaching may be very similar to the leadership style of some leaders. For others it will mean a huge change in their style. If they are usually a very 'top down' leader then staff will be used to being told what to do. They may not adapt to being asked rather then being told that readily.

### KEY POINT

**By coaching people, we are asking them to take responsibility for their own issues and problems.**

If they are used to a set-up where they go to their leader for an answer then they may become very frustrated at having to find one themselves.

There may be a situation when the leader is coaching a member of the team and the team member does not see it as his/her job to come up with his/her own solutions. If there is a dependency on the leader to provide the answers for the team then the coach will have to develop the trust of the learner and show him/her what the benefits of coaching will be.

It is important to make it clear to the learner what the purposes and benefits of coaching are. The learner will develop more skills in the long term and even a renewed sense of purpose for his/her job. Coaching will obviously take more time than just telling someone and involve him/her in taking responsibility but there are benefits in the longer term. The learner may not see this at first and some resistance to coaching may be exhibited. In this kind of situation it is best to start slowly, introducing a few coaching questions gradually.

Let's look at at coaching conversation between Julie and Jack to illustrate this.

## Coaching conversation

Jack is a new team leader and is experiencing some problems with motivating his team. He is used to having half-termly meetings with his line manager, Julie, to get some advice on how to deal with people management issues.

JULIE: Thanks for coming in, Jack. I want to conduct this meeting a bit differently from usual. Do you remember in the staff meeting I said I would be using a coaching approach?

JACK: Oh yes, you have been on a course. That was a few weeks ago. I did not realise we would still be doing that coaching stuff. I thought you would have gone back to the old system by now.

JULIE: No, I am still using the coaching methods. Now tell me, Jack, what do you want to get out of this session?

JACK: What can you do for me? I want some help in dealing with the same old issues. I want to know how I can get Ken to be more receptive and enthusiastic.

JULIE: So how would you like it to be?

JACK: I don't know. I was hoping you would tell me. You have had some good ideas in the past. What shall I do?

JULIE: What is your goal?

JACK: For you to give me some solutions, like you have done in the past. I mean it's fine for you to go on a course but let's get back to normal without the gimmicks. We have not got time for all that. I just want some answers.

JULIE: I am feeling some resistance here, Jack. I understand your frustration. Let's forget the coaching for a moment, just tell me about what happens when Ken kicks off?

JACK: Well he takes any opportunity to have a dig. At team meetings he is always moaning.

JULIE: What does that feel like?

You can see here that Julie has gradually started to introduce coaching questions without Jack realising it. She will eventually get him to form a goal without actually calling it that.

Julie met Jack's resistance by naming it rather than fighting it and carrying on just the same.

97

# Leadership styles

For the purposes of this section we will call a leader anyone who has responsibility for a group of staff within a school. These people will range from subject leaders to admin team leaders to headteachers and the person who is in charge of the lunchtime supervisors. All these people will be using their leadership skills to manage and motivate their staff. In a large secondary school, staff are often members of different teams. You may have a scenario where a person is a team leader in one team and a team member in another. They all have one thing in common: they would benefit from being trained in coaching skills and using them on a day-to-day basis in their leadership roles.

Everyone approaches leadership with his/her own personal style. This will be a combination of elements from his/her own personality and what he/she has seen in term of effective leaders. Leaders we would try to emulate and leaders we would rather forget have influenced us.

A good leader will have a range of leadership styles at his/her fingertips for use in different situations. However, everyone will have a default style, which he/she uses predominately. Many leaders will already be using a coaching style of leadership without even being aware of it. Others will use a more directive approach. There is a continuum of leadership styles and these two styles can be seen at either end.

**Leader as expert** ——————————————————— **Leader as coach**

## Leader as expert

This type of leader will pride him-/herself on knowing everything that is going on in the school or department. He/she will see him-/herself and be seen by staff as having all the answers. When there are problems or solutions these leaders will take a very solution-focused approach to solving them. They like to maintain a great deal of control over the running of the school or department. They have a very 'hands on' approach and are admired for not being prepared to ask anyone to do something they would not be prepared to do themselves. Staff enjoy working for this type of leader because they know exactly where they are with them and expectations are very clear. These leaders are popular with staff because they can get on with the job of teaching, rather than becoming involved in leadership responsibilities. Some staff leave because they see that they are not being developed sufficiently. They feel they are not growing as learners. The leader, as expert, has a very poor work–life balance and he/she sees that as part and parcel of the job. He/she has no time for the strategic side of work, so that is done at home.

At the other end of the continuum we have the leader as coach.

## Leader as coach

This type of leader will maintain an overview of what is going on in the different parts of the school. He/she will never delegate the responsibility for what is going on but have no interest in the minutiae. This leader will rely on the expertise of the team. Problems and issues are regarded as opportunities for learning. These leaders regularly coach staff and develop their skills. Staff enjoy working for this type of leader because they feel valued and trusted to get on with their work. Some staff leave because they see themselves as having too much responsibility.

The leader as coach has a good work–life balance because work has been delegated to staff. He/she has made staff less dependent on him/her, which means that he can get on with the strategic leadership of the school or department, which is seen as his/her job.

Clearly the leader as expert and leader as coach are caricatures made to illustrate a point. Between the two ends of the spectrum there are many variations of leadership style. The two styles do illustrate the fact that the leader as coach has to let go and that can be very worrying.

# Letting go

If you are using a coaching style in your leadership you will have to let go of a number of things. Being right is one of them.

> **KEY POINT**
>
> Remember, you are facilitating the development of your team. They are learning, they are finding out, you are helping them grow. You are not providing answers.

Depending where you are in the continuum given earlier you will have more or less work to do on letting go.

COACHING FOR SCHOOLS

> **KEY POINT**
>
> **If you are building up a coaching culture in your school you will be encouraging staff to experiment. You will be helping people develop ideas. A degree of failure will be expected.**

The leader as coach does not feel the need to be right. If there is a coaching culture in a school, the accent will be on everyone learning. There will be a willingness to share learning and experience.

Looking good is another thing you will have to let go of. If, in a coaching session, you are trying to look good and are concentrating on being skilful, then you are not concentrating on the learner's agenda.

Letting got of solutions is another area to work on. If you are the leader, then probably everyone comes to you to solve his/her problems. You may pride yourself on being able to sort things out. If you are a leader as coach you will focus more on the learning that is taking place than a quick-fix solution. There will be an atmosphere where staff are encouraged to test out ideas. You will be more interested in staff finding their own creative solutions than in providing them yourself. If this is the case then there has to be a no-blame culture.

So, as a leader, you don't tell people what to do, you don't have all the answers, you don't claim to know everything that is going on. What do you do? You do something of a higher order. You coach, delegate, develop, empower and grow staff to work with you. In other words, you view leadership as a collaborative activity.

Collaborative leadership cannot exist in a school where staff are used to the leader as expert. In this situation the staff would not have the skills or expertise to share the leadership. In a set-up with the leader as coach in place, staff will be able to take on the roles and responsibilities that collaborative leadership demands.

## Chapter summary

The main idea to take away from this chapter is that a coaching culture in school will support collaborative leadership. From our case studies we have seen that staff need to be clear about the purpose of coaching before they are trained. Finally, the school with a coaching culture at its heart needs to ensure that its leaders adopt the 'leader as coach' as a leadership style.

## Your learning in practice

What are your actions going to be now?

Write down the most powerful thing you have read so far.

Now what do you need to do about that? Are you going to introduce coaching into your school? Are you going to coach yourself with a triad?

Where are you on the 'leader as coach' continuum?

Place yourself along the scale in terms of:

- leader as expert;
- telling;
- directing;
- showing;
- building up others' confidence;
- tolerating mistakes;
- encouraging;
- empowering;
- leader as coach.

Where are you on this continuum overall?

Where would you like to be?

What does this mean to building up your skill set?

# 5 Coaching to make a difference

This chapter will be relevant to anyone working in a school at any level. Its broad appeal is due to the fact that it centres on the many different applications of coaching to school life. At the heart of this chapter is the fundamental belief that coaching can and will make a positive difference to people's lives at school.

## This chapter in short

We will explore the premise that everyone in a school has huge potential and will look at ways of unlocking that. The process of coaching for confidence will be explored. We will follow a case study showing coaching for confidence-building that will illustrate the huge difference that coaching can make to someone's life and his/her work potential. The chapter will deal with how to just get going with coaching in an informal way. It will also touch on some of the many applications of coaching within a school setting that other chapters have not mentioned. Finally the second case study will follow the setting up of peer coaching in a school.

## Objectives

When you have completed this chapter you will be able to:

- to show how to coach someone in order to increase his/her confidence;

- to illustrate how coaching can release someone's potential;
- to give you the motivation and the tools to get going with coaching;
- to illustrate how peer coaching can be used as highly effective professional development for staff;
- to explore how coaching can be used with teachers, children, parents and governors.

## Coaching and realising potential

Everyone has great untapped potential, some of which is realised through work and some of it is left latent and untapped. There are some people who blossom in a work situation. School as a place of work suits their natural talents and abilities. Alternatively, there are always people at school who do not seem that committed to their work or who are not very enthusiastic about achieving anything inside school but have very absorbing and demanding hobbies. These people's achievements outside of school can be really spectacular but at work they are content to remain in the background.

Then there are other people whose potential is not realised until there is a crisis. People who seem reluctant to accept responsibility at work may do really well heading up a situation in an emergency and use skills they did not realise that they had.

People at work who are achieving their potential will be happy to take on new projects. These projects will constantly test their skill levels. They may even work well beyond their level of capability. They relish the challenge of a new task and seek out new responsibilities. They do not necessarily have the knowledge and skills to carry out these new tasks but what they do have is the self-belief that they can do it. They will take risks and trust that all will turn out well. They will have an inflated idea of their own capabilities and may be a bit shocked that they are actually finding some tasks harder than they assumed. They underestimate what is involved in a new task and sometimes have to backtrack, slowing down the pace of the task. They leave quite a few things to chance rather than plan in advance. This can lead to tasks not being completed and high degrees of stress. People who are not achieving their potential will be playing safe. They will make sure that everything they do is well within their skill levels. They will try to carry out projects that they have done before or are similar. Any new task they undertake will be planned in great detail. They will want a detailed description of what is going to happen before they undertake anything new. They will constantly underestimate their abilities. They may be totally unaware that they have the ability to achieve more. They will have put limitations around themselves and what they are capable of. They will be happy operating within their comfort zone. These people can be very skilled at what they do but they lack the confidence to try new areas and will take a lot of support and mentoring to operate in a different way. Whether staff are realising their potential or not, coaching will help them to work more effectively.

So let us look at what is it that gets in the way of people realising their true potential.

As a coach you first of all have to believe that the performance someone is putting in at work is not necessarily all they are capable of. It is important to see beyond that with some people, otherwise you will be missing what they are truly able to do. You need to be careful not to define someone by their performance but look beyond that to their capabilities. If someone can train for and run the London Marathon in their spare time then that shows they have determination and inner reserves. This same person at work may put up a lot of resistance to learning new skills. Surely that person can apply their determination to learning some new computer skills and master the intricacies of Excel or Access. This person may need coaching to unlock that store of motivation that he/she is keeping for running and apply it to the work setting.

Coaching someone is about getting the best from them. If you are going to get the best from them you need to first believe that the best is there. Very often all someone needs to develop their potential is someone who believes in them. Coaching provides that series of one-to-one, structured conversations to move someone forward.

### KEY POINT

Coaching is about looking beyond a person's performance and seeing his/her potential. To coach someone you need to believe in him/her.

## Coaching to build confidence

The case study that we are about to explore is about an adult working in a secondary school. However, both the principles and the process can be applied to children as well. As someone working in a school you will be dedicated to improving the lives of young people. You will be able to spot the child with potential in your groups and classes, the child who has very low self-esteem and just needs someone to believe in them and coach them to be able to achieve. We know that for children self-belief is a vital ingredient to becoming a successful learner. It is equally important for adults, as the following case study will illustrate.

## Case study

Name of school: Castle Park School. A large secondary with 1,100 pupils on roll.

Context: A successful inner-city school with Sports College Specialist status. Attainment is average when compared to similar schools and there is a large sixth form.

Background: There is a staff of 100 full- and part-time teaching staff and 20 teaching assistants. There are 6 admin staff led by the bursar and the entire full- and-part time staff number is 150. Kevin, the bursar, has undergone some coaching training along with other team leaders within the school. He is meeting his team members once a month to coach them on their professional roles. We are going to follow Kevin as he coaches Sandra. Sandra is an admin assistant whose role has grown enormously over the ten years she has worked at the school. She started work at the school as a lunchtime supervisor, when her children attended the school, and then began to work in the office. She has shown a lot of ability with figures and has mastered the school's finance software easily. Sandra comes over as someone who is very quiet and does not put herself forward for any training or extra tasks. Kevin has been frustrated recently as he has asked Sandra to train other staff in the finance software and she has seemed very reluctant. At home Sandra is addicted to Sudoku puzzles and does the most complicated ones in no time at all. Despite this talent, she will not enter the staffroom Sudoku challenge that takes place every term. Kevin senses that Sandra has a lot of potential and could get extra qualifications and he cannot figure out what is holding back someone so able. There was also a recent INSET day when she became upset and left the group session.

COACHING FOR SCHOOLS

This is Sandra's first session with Kevin.

## Coaching conversation

KEVIN: Sandra, thanks for coming in. You know that we are going to have these sessions once a month and we are going to set a professional goal together and work on it throughout the year. Is that OK?

SANDRA: Yes, OK. Is it a bit like the old performance management?

KEVIN: Yes it is but I am going to regularly coach you on your PM targets. Before we start on that, I want to raise something with you. I notice that on the software package training day, when we were all sat in the circle, you were not happy about that. Is there anything you would like to discuss?

SANDRA: I do not like anything like that... in a group. I knew I would have to say something. I could not do that.

KEVIN: What was it that you could not do?

SANDRA: I could not speak in front of everyone. We all had to say what we wanted to get out of the day and I couldn't think of what to say.

KEVIN: How did it make you feel?

SANDRA: I just wanted the earth to swallow me up. I don't like everyone looking at me. I can't talk in front of everyone. I just can't. Now I feel even worse because I have made a fool of myself in front of everyone and they are all wondering what is wrong.

KEVIN: You were not happy talking out loud in front of everyone. What would you have been happy with?

SANDRA: I would not have minded telling the person next to me and then reporting back as a pair to the group. That would have been fine.

KEVIN: So it wasn't coming up with the answer to 'What are you expecting from the day?' that worried you?

SANDRA: No not at all. I knew the answer to that. I was looking forward to getting some of my queries about the software sorted out and learning some new shortcuts. I just didn't want to be put on the spot in front of everyone, looking stupid.

KEVIN: Looking stupid to whom?

SANDRA: I don't know. To the others I suppose. They all seem so confident. I always have had a problem with being in the limelight. I don't like people looking at me. I don't like the focus on me.

KEVIN: What happens when the focus is on you?

SANDRA: All my confidence goes. I feel small and inadequate. That's why I have not wanted to train that group of new teaching assistants. When you asked me to do part of their induction, I just died. I don't like talking to more than one person at a time. I also don't want them looking at me thinking 'What does she know?' I would be terrified of making a mess of it.

KEVIN: What learning did you take away from the INSET day?

SANDRA: That I should not be so stupid. I know that I am just as good as anyone else but I can't seem to get past that barrier of speaking in a group.

KEVIN: Is that something that you would like to work on?

SANDRA: Yes it is. I feel it is holding me back. I would like to do that training you asked me about with the new teaching assistants but I have to sort this out first.

## How coaching helped

This session helped Sandra realise that it was her lack of confidence that was holding her back. Kevin had previously wondered why she did not want to get involved with inducting the new teaching assistants and had assumed that Sandra was just being uncooperative. It also made Kevin think again about the planning of INSET days. He had been oblivious to the fact that anyone would feel threatened by having to speak in a group and would plan the next day differently.

The session made Sandra challenge herself and think about why she could not speak in a group. Through talking to Kevin she realised that her lack of confidence was holding her back and she wanted to do something about it.

Sandra formulated a goal with Kevin which was: *To talk confidently in front of a small group.* Kevin and Sandra planned together a series of small steps towards

COACHING FOR SCHOOLS

this. Kevin recognised that Sandra was someone who liked to be very well prepared for everything she did, so he allowed time in the plan of action for Sandra to plan every step. To Kevin this seemed highly unnecessary but it was Sandra's goal and she needed to tackle it in her own way.

Over time Sandra explained the new finance system first to an individual and then to a pair of staff and so on. The school decided to go over to keeping their pupil attainment data on the same system, which meant that Sandra then had to explain the system to teachers. This seemed like another hurdle to her, as she had previously only dealt with other admin staff. Kevin and Sandra agreed, in the next coaching session, that Sandra would start by just explaining the new system to a pair of teachers using the same format as with the admin staff.

The session took place with the teachers and it did not go well. Sandra became so nervous that she was not able to train the teachers on interrogating the data. Everyone was very sympathetic, but Sandra found the whole experience demoralising and we join Kevin and Sandra in their coaching session shortly after the disastrous training session.

### Coaching conversation

KEVIN: You have had the training session with Kate and Barbara.

SANDRA: Yes, it went really badly. I was a wreck. I can't stop asking myself 'Why did it happen?' I just went to pieces. I have really gone backwards in terms of my goal; I may as well forget it.

KEVIN: I do not really want to focus on why it happened with the teachers. Let's look to the future.

SANDRA: Don't you think we should analyse what went wrong. Talk about it, try and figure out why?

KEVIN: No, I would like to focus on what has gone right since the last session. What has worked well?

SANDRA: That's difficult, all I can think of is that awful session with Kate and Barbara. Um...(silence)...I suppose that I did have that session with the two teaching assistants that went well, but with the teachers I have not got the confidence. I am not a confident person.

KEVIN: You are not a confident person. Can I make a suggestion?

SANDRA: Yes.

108

KEVIN: I suggest that 'I am not a confident person' is a belief that you have about yourself rather than a fact. It is a belief that you have learned.

SANDRA: I don't understand.

KEVIN: Well you were not born believing that you are not confident at work.

SANDRA: OK.

KEVIN: This belief is something that you have learned over time. Every time something saps your confidence, the belief becomes more entrenched. The good news is that this belief you have about yourself can be changed.

SANDRA: So what you're saying is I can learn to be more confident.

KEVIN: Yes. Can you think of a situation where you are confident?

SANDRA: Yes, I am confident at home and in situations where I know that I can do something.

KEVIN: If I gave you one of those Sudoku puzzles to finish, how would you treat that?

SANDRA: OK yes, with confidence. Because I am good at it, I have done it before. I suppose it comes back to my goal. I am not confident in front of groups of people.

KEVIN: Are you still happy with your goal: 'To talk confidently in front of a small group'?

SANDRA: It is more than that. It is about my general confidence at work. I am not a confident person at work.

KEVIN: What would you get if you changed this belief about yourself?

SANDRA: I would be able to tackle new things with confidence, without stress and nerves. I would feel as if there was nothing holding me back. I would be ready to learn and develop my skills.

KEVIN: If I could give you this belief now would you take it?

SANDRA: (Without hesitation) YES!

KEVIN: So what would it be helpful to believe about yourself?

SANDRA: That I am a person who is confident at work.

> KEVIN: Good, can you turn that into a process, for instance bring in a verb? For instance, I can learn or I can try to be.
>
> SANDRA: Do you mean like 'I can learn how to be person who is confident at work'?
>
> KEVIN: Yes, good. Now can you add a word to that which is going to make it more pleasurable for you, such as enjoy or have fun.
>
> SANDRA: 'I can enjoy learning how to be a person who is confident at work'.

## How coaching helped

In the first coaching session with Kevin, Sandra realised that it was her confidence that was holding her back. In the second session, Kevin identified that her lack of confidence at work was a deep-seated limiting belief that she had about herself. It was not a fact but a belief that could be changed. The other feature of the coaching session was that it did not focus on the past. Kevin at no point tried to analyse what went wrong and he never asked the question 'Why?'

### KEY POINT

**Coaching is always future-focused and never analyses the past.**

## Further work to change a limiting belief

Kevin gave Sandra some work to do before the next session on her new belief, 'I can enjoy learning how to be a person who is confident at work'.

He gave her a sheet with the following tasks on it.

1. Write down your new belief and notice any feelings or self-talk that comes up which may object to it.
2. Let these objections go by writing them down. Now throw them away. These objections have moved from being subconscious to being conscious and have been acknowledged and dealt with.
3. Take a minute to imagine yourself living for a day with this belief. What would it feel like? What would you be hearing, seeing and doing?

4. The thoughts and feelings that you used to answer 3 are now your anchor and you need to start each day with the thoughts and feelings that go along with being confident at work.

At the next session with Kevin, Sandra formulated a confidence plan, as follows.

| **Confidence plan: Sandra O'Neil**  **Date:** |
|---|
| Goal: 'I can enjoy learning how to be a person who is confident at work' |
| What drains my confidence and how can I avoid it? |
| What situations am I confident in? |
| What strategies can I bring from home to make me more confident? |
| Who can I get help from to build my confidence? |
| How can I build in milestones in increasing my confidence that I can celebrate? |

This confidence plan enabled Sandra to identify times when she could learn successfully and feel confident: in other words, when she was in a state of what we call 'FLOW'. Adults will learn when they feel relaxed and confident. Sandra was able to pinpoint that she was best able to learn at home. She felt relaxed and confident to do those Sudoku puzzles and she needed to replicate that state of 'FLOW' at work. She needed to be challenged but not too much. Like most people, she worked best when she was challenged but not overwhelmed by the task.

COACHING FOR SCHOOLS

> **Exercise**
>
> Think about Kevin's work on coaching for confidence with Sandra and see how it could be adapted to work with children. Think of a child who would benefit from a confidence plan and how you would adapt it to suit the needs of a young person.

**Case study conclusion**

Kevin continued to work with Sandra over a year and her confidence at work did grow. She went on to regularly contribute to the induction programme for new staff. She also conquered her fear of speaking in large groups and ended up running a small group training session in an INSET day. Sandra blossomed at work and at the end of the year had signed up with the local training provider to do a course in business administration.

Kevin asked for some feedback from all of his team on the coaching he had given and the following is what Sandra had written:

> When I came to work at the school I thought I had reached my ceiling. I was on the edge of doing all that I was capable of. You have helped me realise that I am capable of so much more. I was never very successful at school and came from a home where praise was not used very much. The coaching sessions with you have given me so much confidence and made me realise what I can really do. You did not do this for me, but you made me do it myself and I am so proud of that.

Coaching is rewarding work and represents a huge investment in people. Not only did Sandra benefit from these sessions but Kevin also grew in confidence as a coach. Kevin has now spotted the potential in Sandra to learn coaching skills herself so that she can coach the new teaching assistants and he hopes that will be in next year's plan.

# Peer coaching

We have looked, in our case study, at how coaching can be applied in a team leader/team member scenario. In the case study Kevin was the team leader. He was in a senior position and was more experienced in his job than Sandra. Part of his role as team leader was to coach Sandra.

COACHING TO MAKE A DIFFERENCE

Now let's explore a situation in which the coach and the learner are equal in status and experience.

Peer coaching is when two members of staff form a coaching pair. The pair have agreed to support each other in their professional learning through peer coaching. Peer coaching will provide the coaching pair with an opportunity for self-evaluation of their own teaching. It will also give them the chance for some professional development, not only in what they will learn from their partner but also in developing their own coaching skills. Peer coaching provides the coaching pair with a very practical and powerful way of learning about their own and each other's teaching.

## Case study

Name of school: Maize Primary School. A large primary with 350 pupils on roll plus a 45-place nursery.

Context: A successful inner-city school that is part of an Education Action Zone (EAZ). Attainment is below average when compared to similar schools and there is a huge drive throughout the EAZ to increase standards of attainment. The LA is failing and the schools have built up a collaborative network through the EAZ that has been far more influential and useful to the schools than the LA.

Background: The EAZ runs a programme of coaching and training for coaching. Two Year 3 teachers at Maize Primary, Peter and Glynnis, have been on a coaching course and are eager to start some peer coaching. They have approached the headteacher with their ideas, seeking her support. The headteacher is already receiving executive coaching from the EAZ and has seen how powerful it is. She is sympathetic to the idea of peer coaching but is worried that the staff have enough initiatives to cope with currently. She has given Glynnis and Peter the go-ahead to start peer coaching in a small way as long as it relates directly to one of the school's goals from the School Improvement Plan (SIP).

The school has introduced a programme of thinking skills with the children in an effort to increase standards. It is also working on making the curriculum more creative. It is these initiatives that Peter and Glynnis wish to focus on in their peer coaching.

To make their project successful the headteacher was able to allocate a small amount of supply time from the EAZ funding. To justify this she required that ▶

Glynnis and Peter come up with a plan. Glynnis and Peter discussed their plans and decided that it was really important to establish not only what they would do but also the principles behind it.

---

Below is the document that they came up with.

**Peer coaching plan for Maize Primary School**

Links to School Improvement Plan: Goal 3, to raise standards in teaching and learning through the 'Learning to learn' strategies.

Peer coaching objectives:
- to share best practice;
- to be able to reflect upon and refine our own practice;
- to provide ongoing mutual support;
- to establish a professional dialogue together;
- to provide each other with specific feedback;
- to foster a culture of collaboration.

Peer coaching principles:
- it is non-evaluative and non-judgemental;
- it is based on a trusting relationship between two members of staff;
- it is done in a confidential way;
- it is done in a non-threatening secure environment;
- both teachers aim to grow together.

Method:
- both teachers will use PPA time, during which they will plan together to decide which lessons will be selected;
- the particular focus of the peer observation will be determined by the teacher being observed but is within the focus of the SIP's Goal 3, to raise standards in teaching and learning through the 'Learning to learn' strategies;
- time for feedback for the observations will be on the same day that the lesson took place and will be covered by the part-time teacher funded by the EAZ.

Evaluation:
- both teachers will produce a report for the headteacher and governors in six months' time.

Glynnis and Peter had received coaching training from an EAZ training day. They were familiar with the LEAP model, which they had used a couple of times, and they had done some work on listening and questioning skills. They were both conscious that the LEAP model would need adapting for peer coaching.

1. *Looking at goals*

   This stage would be covered in the pre-lesson discussion, during which the objectives of the lesson would be discussed. The goal would be the part of the lesson that the teacher would want the teacher/coach to focus on. For instance, a goal could be 'To ensure that all children make good use of their learning diaries'.

2. *Exploring reality*

   This stage would take place in the after-lesson coaching session. The teacher coach would be asking questions like 'What do you think happened in the lesson?', 'What were the most effective parts of the lesson in terms of your goal?' They would then be sharing their own observations of the lesson.

3. *Analysing possibilities*

   In this stage the teacher/coach would encourage the teacher to think of all the different ways in which he/she could work towards the goals with the children. The teacher/coach would also give some ideas of his/her own at this point. In coaching we normally say the coach should avoid saying 'I would do it this way'. Peer coaching is a little bit different. One of the objectives is about sharing good practice. It is acceptable in this context for the teacher/coach to share what has worked in his/her classroom after the teacher, who is being coached, has come up with his/her own ideas.

4. *Planning for action*

   At this stage the teacher/coach is asking questions such as 'What could you do?' and 'Who could you ask?' or 'What might you need to help you?' The teacher being coached will come up with an action plan that will inform the next goal. Let us join Glynnis and Peter at one of their coaching sessions after a lesson. Glynnis is the coach and Peter has been observed. The focus of the observation was the theme of teaching children what to do if they get stuck on something while working. This is a theme running through the whole school's project on thinking skills. The teachers have been trying to teach the children to become more resilient and use problem-solving techniques instead of just getting stuck or simply asking the teacher.

Remember that the *Looking at goals* stage of the LEAP model had already been covered in the pre-lesson planning session. The lesson was on numeracy.

# COACHING FOR SCHOOLS

## Coaching conversation

GLYNNIS: So Peter, in terms of your goal, how did you feel the lesson went?

PETER: Well, I was a bit disappointed that they did not remember the strategies that we discussed last time. Although the blue group got on really well, it does seem that the bright ones have no trouble learning about strategies to help them learn but the ones who need more help find it more of a problem.

GLYNNIS: What was it with the blue group that worked?

PETER: Well, they used their learning diaries to refer back to strategies that they had used to solve problems before. It was magic really. I did not even have to remind them. I was really pleased. Not only that, they added to the learning diaries at the end of the lesson.

GLYNNIS: Yes, I noticed that. Did you also realise that the yellow group also conferred with each other on what problem-solving strategies each person used?

PETER: No, I missed that. Did you notice anything else?

GLYNNIS: Well, if you take the class as a whole, I was impressed with the resourcefulness that they demonstrated. A good proportion, say 60 per cent, were using their learning diaries. There were others having a really good dialogue about learning, using some of the vocabulary that we have taught them. If you take the class as a whole I would say that 80 per cent were using some sort of behaviours associated with good learners. You have done well with them. I really like the way that you refer to the learning diaries and make them part of the lesson. I have never been able to do that.

PETER: That is so interesting. I would never have said that. I was so concerned with the red group not being able to use the problem-solving strategies that I did not get an overall impression of the lesson and how the class was tackling it. Although I am pleased with what you are saying I am still worried about the red group.

GLYNNIS: OK. What could you try with them?

PETER: They need some sort of scaffolding with the 'What to do if you are stuck' strategies. We have been over them. They don't seem able to use their learning diaries: they have not got anything in them.

GLYNNIS: Do they have to have learning diaries?

PETER: Well, it is whole-school policy that every child has one, but I suppose that there is no point if they don't use them. Maybe something else would be more appropriate... Perhaps some visual symbols in the front of their books. You know, one picture for 'Split up the question', one for 'Ask someone else'. Have you got any ideas?

GLYNNIS: Yes. There is one thing I do with my low-ability group. We made a list as a class of all the strategies we use when we get stuck and we put them on a set of laminated cards. Then we made a container for them; the children call it the 'stuck box'. When anyone is stuck they just go and get a card out of the 'stuck box' and it reminds them of what they could do.

PETER: That's really good. The process of thinking of the strategies is worth doing with them for a start and then we could devise some visual symbols for each strategy to help them remember. So the cards in the 'stuck box' could have visual symbols as well. I like that.

GLYNNIS: Well, what I am going to take away from your lesson is using the learning diaries. I am going to try and weave them into the lesson as you did, so that they become second nature. That has been my learning point.

## How coaching helped

Glynnis was able to supply Peter with factual non-judgemental feedback on the lesson. Peter benefited from this because he was so absorbed in teaching the lesson and solving the problems of the red group that he did not have an accurate overview of what was happening in the lesson overall.

Glynnis was able to provide non-evaluative feedback on the lesson and was able to hone in on exactly what Peter asked her to look at. Peter was left with some strategies and ideas to help the red group that arose out of his coaching session with Glynnis. This is powerful and practical learning for Peter.

The other thing that happened was that the learning was a two-way process: Glynnis also learned from watching Peter and will adapt her practice accordingly.

We usually say that in a coaching situation the coach should do no more than 30 per cent of the talking. It is a little bit different in peer coaching and it can become more of a dialogue. The teacher/coach still has to make sure that he/she does not dominate the coaching session with suggestions. It is vital that both the teacher/coach and the teacher being observed make explicit what their learning was from the lesson. They also both need to record how their practice will change as a result.

## Case study conclusion

Over the six months, Glynnis and Peter managed to watch three of each other's lessons and have had follow-up coaching sessions. They considered it a great success and produced the following report for the headteacher and governors.

### Peer coaching project, Maize Primary School by Glynnis Clarke and Peter Hutchinson

What went well?
- We feel that we have become learners. We feel that through doing this we have become better role models for the children because we are evaluating our own practice.
- We feel less isolated as professionals.
- This has helped us on our Performance Management targets, which are related to the SIP's Goal 3 to raise standards in teaching and learning through the 'Learning to learn' strategies.
- We have opened up a debate about learning and teaching in the staffroom.
- Other staff are interested in what we are doing and there is much more of a spirit of collaboration than before.
- We both feel we have gained in confidence as teachers and as coaches.
- We both feel that the quality of teaching and learning has increased in our classrooms and the pupils have directly benefited.

What would have made it even better?
- If we had decided beforehand on a pro forma for the follow-up coaching sessions.
- If we had put more emphasis on the coach learning from the teacher being coached.
- If we had shared with the classes from the outset what we were doing.

The headteacher was so impressed with the outcomes of the project that she decided to build peer coaching into the next year's SIP and adopt it throughout the school. Glynnis and Peter would train all staff on coaching and how to set it up. As a successful piece of professional development, the peer coaching project had been relatively inexpensive. The headteacher hoped that it would help build a more collaborative culture within the school.

Having looked in detail at coaching for confidence and peer coaching we are now going to move on to briefly examine some other uses of coaching.

**Chapter summary**

The belief that coaching can make a difference has been at the heart of this chapter. We have seen how coaching has improved someone's confidence at work and empowered them to overcome the barriers that were holding them back from reaching their potential at work. We have also seen how peer coaching has been used as a powerful tool to make learners out of teachers. Finally we have touched on a few further applications of coaching and explored ways of getting started.

# Learning review

What has been the most powerful thing that you have learned from this chapter? How is it going to change your practice at work? What do you need to do to make coaching happen for you? What is your next step?

# 6 Coaching and performance management

This chapter will be of interest to anyone involved in performance management. That includes anyone who is carrying it out as a team leader or anyone who is on the receiving end of it as a team member.

## This chapter in short

This chapter will look at how you can improve your performance management system by using coaching skills and techniques. For team leaders it will provide valuable help on giving feedback. For team members it will help you in self-assessment and receiving feedback. It will also look at turning performance management objectives into meaningful goals.

## Objectives

When you have completed this chapter you will be able to:

- promote the self-assessment of performance and provide a framework for it;
- examine the skills of giving and receiving feedback;
- look at how to get the best from people;
- look at how to get the best from the school;
- examine ways of dealing with blockages that stop people from developing.

## What is performance management?

If performance management is a tool for measuring performance, then we must first decide what performance is. There are many different ways of measuring performance with regard to teaching. Some schools may see it as good test results, others good discipline. Both Ofsted and Hay McBer have standard features of a good lesson. Something for your school to think about is what you have decided the measures are of good performance.

There are standards already decided by the Training and Development Agency (TDA) that we can use to measure performance. There are standards for higher-level teaching assistants, subject leaders, teachers and headteachers. These standards ought to be used as benchmarks for people's own self-assessment. A checklist of these standards would be an excellent starting point for any self-assessment. (See http://www.tda.gov.uk/leaders/leadershipsupport/standardsframework.aspx for more information on these standards.)

## The purposes of performance management

The performance management (PM) cycle has been in schools since 2000. In many schools it is now well established and embedded and, yet, what has its impact been on both school and personal development?

This is not easily measured, but let's reflect for a moment. Clearly, performance management is a valuable tool for schools. It should be at the heart of the school's development. Everyone in a school will perform better when they feel valued and appreciated. Making staff feel like this should be one of the main objectives of the performance management cycle. That's why it is essential that every member of staff is involved in some sort of system. It is everyone's right to know how he/she is getting on at work. If non-teaching staff are left out of this valuable process then it creates an unfair two-tier system. A school is an organic institution where all the parts fit together for the good of the children. There would be little point in one section feeling valued and developed and the other section feeling demotivated.

Think about how performance management works in your school. How much is your PM cycle a part of your school's strategic development? It could be totally integrated into your school improvement cycle or perhaps it is just an add-on activity that is squeezed into the beginning and end of your academic year. An effective PM cycle can move the school forward, so, looking at the

COACHING FOR SCHOOLS

following checklist, let's see how your school measures up. Check if your PM cycle includes the following:

- alignment of personal goals to school goals;
- all non-teaching staff included in a performance management cycle;
- all team members encouraged to think about their own self-assessment before review meetings;
- everyone collecting their own evidence base to use at PM interviews;
- regular coaching and training for team leaders in giving and receiving feedback.

Reflect for a moment on the above points. What issues do they raise with you, what are the weak areas that they reveal?

If you have any weak areas at all then I suggest that you read on.

## The performance management cycle

The DfES circular 0051/2000 identifies three phases in the performance management cycle.

- **Planning:** team leaders discuss and record priorities and objectives with each of the teachers in their team. They discuss how progress will be monitored.
- **Monitoring:** the teacher and team leader keep progress under review throughout the cycle, taking any supportive action needed.
- **Review:** the teacher and the team leader review achievements over the year and evaluate the teacher's overall performance taking account of progress against objectives.

### KEY POINT

Using coaching techniques at each stage of the performance management cycle will make the system more meaningful and rigorous.

Let's look at the three stages of the cycle and see where coaching can help.

**Phase one**
**Planning**
Goal-setting    Aligning personal    Action planning    Self-assessment
                and school goals

# The planning stage

Each one of the above phases named by the DfES will require a meeting or an activity. The planning phase will be best served by a meeting.

## Preparation for the planning meeting

Time spent in this meeting will be richer and more productive if the members of staff have done some thinking beforehand. Some sort of self-assessment against agreed criteria needs to take place during this time. All staff need to have ownership of this meeting and be made to feel that they are being proactive rather than told what to do.

Before the planning meeting each member of staff needs time to fill in a questionnaire. Part of this questionnaire will identify his/her roles and responsibilities. It will also ask him/her to reflect on what is going well in his/her job and what needs developing.

Prior to the meeting it is important to establish what that person does in school. This may sound a bit obvious, but it is surprising how roles and responsibilities change in school. This can happen gradually as internal roles get re-allocated.

For example, when Susan – the NQT mentor of a small primary school – left to go on maternity leave, Terry said he would step in and take on the role. Terry was already maths and geography coordinator. When it was decided that Susan was not coming back it seemed to be taken for granted that Terry would carry on with his new role, plus the others.

Also, let's look at Sandra who works in an expanding City Technical College. She is a higher-level teaching assistant who was asked to take over the induction of other teaching assistants at short notice. Now, six months later, she is still doing it and, as there are a lot of new staff, it is quite a large job.

Both Terry and Sandra are approaching their planning meetings with their team leaders and they are worried about being held accountable for these new responsibilities for which they have had no training.

That is why a question like 'What are your major roles and responsibilities?' is essential in the pre-meeting questionnaire.

The questionnaire also needs to give an opportunity for some self-coaching. The person needs to be prompted into thinking about what their strengths are and their development needs. It is important that they also think of ways in which these could be addressed.

The questions listed below for the pre-planning questionnaire will encourage the member of staff to take a more proactive approach to the whole process and it will enable the team leader to take a coaching approach with them. Part of the self-assessment before the meeting would be to use the TDA's national standards to highlight strengths and area of weakness.

Here are some examples of self-assessment questions.

- What are your major roles and responsibilities?
- What is your greatest strength/talent?
- How is that being used?
- What is your greatest area of weakness in your job?
- How does that become apparent?
- What have you tried already to rectify that weakness?
- What is getting in the way of you developing this area?
- What are the strategies/tools that could assist you in this area?
- What training have you been on already relating your role?

## The planning meeting

> **KEY POINT**
>
> Using coaching questions during the planning meeting will give the learner more ownership of the process.

If the above questions have been answered then there is every chance that the meeting will be rich and purposeful. With the preparatory work done, the focus of this meeting should be on goal-setting. However, life being as it is and staff being human beings, this is not always the case.

One of the pitfalls of performance management is that it can become a moaning session and a lot of negativity from staff can be experienced. Some people are reluctant to being coached and resistant to change and it will take some skill from the team leader to handle them.

For example, let's take Natalie. Natalie is a senior early year's practitioner working in an early year's excellence centre. The following coaching conversation took place during a planning meeting stage of the PM cycle.

## Coaching conversation

COACH: Natalie, thanks for filling in the questionnaire. I see from your sheet that, since Ken left, you now have responsibility for students.

NATALIE: Yes.

COACH: And of all your responsibilities this is the one that is causing you the most concern.

NATALIE: Yes, it is just not fair. I already have more to do than any of the other seniors and this was just plonked in my pigeon hole without warning. I really should not be doing it, I have enough with home/school liaison and all the other stuff that I do.

COACH: Which particular bit of dealing with students do you find difficult?

NATALIE: All of it. They come in with their portfolios and their tasks, they seem to have no idea of what is expected, their tutors hardly speak to me. I should not be doing it. Ken was a teacher; he had had more experience. This is not the sort of job I should be doing. I did not become a nursery nurse for this.

COACH: Under 'What have you tried already?' – in the questionnaire – you have put that you have already had a conversation with the centre manager about whose responsibility this is.

NATALIE: Yes and I got nowhere, she did not listen. I am stuck with it and I should not be doing it.

COACH: Is there anything you could try?

NATALIE: Yes, I could try talking to Sheila and seeing if she wants to take it on; she is so keen.

COACH: So how could we move forward on this?

NATALIE: Get someone else to do it.

You can clearly see that Natalie is entrenched with the idea that dealing with students is not her job. She is finding it very difficult to move beyond that. Even when the coach asked her what she had tried she interpreted it to mean: 'How have you tried to get rid of it?'

## Dealing with resistance

Natalie is going to be very resistant to setting goals and developing her role with responsibility for students.

Let's look at the possible reasons:

- she does not like change;
- she is worried about failing;
- she does not want to come out of her comfort zone;
- she feels threatened by the tutors;
- she does not see herself as confident in the role.

The truth is it is probably a combination of all of the above that is preventing her from moving forward.

The skill of the coach here is to enable Natalie to see beyond the immediate problem of this role. She needs to recognise that if she could develop her skills in this area it would be of long-term benefit for her.

The coach needs to do the following:

- establish and clarify the scope and purpose of this role;
- find out exactly what is happening;
- uncover what the key areas of skill are that need developing;
- enable her to write a goal;
- work out the support that Natalie will need;
- agree an action plan and secure Natalie's commitment.

You can see immediately the four stages of the LEAP model coming through. The *Looking at goals* stage in this instance has come second rather than first and the *Exploring reality* stage has come first. This is a good example of how the LEAP model can be adapted to suit the situation.

So, let's see how the coach is getting on with Natalie. Their conversation has continued and they have established what the role entails. Natalie has agreed, reluctantly, that she will need to work on developing this role, as there is no one else to take it on in the foreseeable future. The coach has agreed that they will fully review the roles and responsibilities of all the senior early year's practitioners in six months' time.

# COACHING AND PERFORMANCE MANAGEMENT

## Coaching conversation

COACH: So, Natalie, which bits of the student role do you find the most challenging?

NATALIE: The dealing with the tutors... actually, and the students — they do not seem to know what is expected and they leave everything to the last minute.

COACH: OK, let's deal with the students first. What could you do?

NATALIE: I could try to get hold of their schedule of tasks from the college and go through it with them when they start.

COACH: Good, what else?

NATALIE: I could just tell them that it is not my job to chase them and they have to plan their work. In fact if I held a meeting with them and laid this on the line and put up their schedule on the wall and gave them a copy, then they would have to manage it themselves.

COACH: Natalie I am really impressed with that. Good, that's really positive. Now what about the tutors?

NATALIE: This is not so easy. They don't respect me like they respected Ken. I do not feel comfortable talking to them. They are always in a hurry, I don't know when they are going to turn up and they expect me to have time to talk to them.

COACH: So you don't feel respected. How does that show?

NATALIE: Well, if they respected me, they would make a proper appointment and then I would be prepared and more confident about their visit. The trouble is, I can't ask them to make an appointment. I am only a nursery nurse, I can't speak to them like that. What will they think?

COACH: Only a nursery nurse?

NATALIE: Yes, well, OK, an early year's administrator with responsibility for students. Yes I know I should really try to deal with it. I should be able to talk to them as equals. It's just that if I felt more confident with the role then I could do it.

So the real issue has been uncovered. What was stopping Natalie moving forward was the following:

- lack of clarity about the role;
- lack of confidence in dealing with tutors;
- limiting beliefs about herself.

> **KEY POINT**
>
> Whenever people say: 'I'm only a ...' you know that they have a limiting belief about themselves. They have put limitations around what they can and cannot do.

The coach did some work with Natalie on her lack of confidence. They also discussed how she saw herself. The coach tried to get Natalie to imagine herself in situations where she did feel confident. They came to the conclusion that it was when she was in a situation where everything was highly structured. This gave the coach an opportunity to build on. So it was decided to bring more structure into the meetings with the tutors. This would make Natalie feel more in control.

The coach then went on to work with Natalie on a goal relating to feeling more assertive in dealing with the tutors. They then worked on an action plan and agreed to review it at intervals during the year. It was also agreed that Natalie would get some support and training in leadership skills.

# Setting objectives

This is a crucial part of the planning stage and many of the skills and techniques used in *Looking at goals* are useful here.

After clarifying the roles and responsibilities, the next focus of the planning phase is the priorities for the next year. The discussion on priorities needs to focus on the needs of the pupils and the member of staff. It is important to have a copy of the school development plan available during this discussion, so that it can provide a broader context for the objectives. The member of staff will have to set an objective on pupil progress. However, this objective may not necessarily relate to test results.

If, for instance, the school's main focus for development in that year was to make the pupils more independent in their work, the teacher could have an objective focused on that. The school will have already worked out what they mean by independent learning in their training. So they will have an idea of what a classroom full of independent workers looks like. Given this, then classroom observations will be a good way to measure progress.

The objectives need to highlight the main expectations that the member of staff has for the following year in terms of him-/herself and his/her pupils. Like goals, objectives need to be SMART and flexible. During the year a number of factors may change and objectives may need reviewing. There is no hard-and-fast rule about how many objectives a person may have – between three and five seems ideal.

It is important that the coach involves the member of staff in the writing of these objectives, that they are easily understood and that the assessment of them is going to be transparent.

Let's look at how a coaching conversation was used to help write a pupil progress objective in a planning phase meeting.

## Coaching conversation

Mark is a Year 8 maths teacher in an inner-city secondary school in London.

COACH: Now Mark, I see from your self-assessment form that you have identified improving the NFER [National Foundation for Educational Research] maths scores of all your groups at the end of the year as your pupil progress objective for this year.

MARK: Yes.

COACH: That's quite a broad goal, can we narrow it down a bit?

MARK: But I want all the pupils to do well.

COACH: Of course. Which group of pupils do you think are making the least progress?

MARK: Well, according to the data it is the English as a second language children who are not doing as well as the others.

COACH: So is that a group we could focus your goal on.

MARK: We could but that does not mean that I am not going to work hard with the others.

COACH: OK, now what are the key themes of the school development plan this year?

> MARK: It's raising standards, it is always raising standards... but this year we are looking particularly at ethnic groups and raising their achievement. This ties in well with what I want to do.
>
> COACH: Good, so can we begin to phrase a goal?
>
> MARK: Yes, what about 'To do an audit of the EAL children and find out what their problems are in maths', whether it is the comprehension of subject-specific language perhaps?
>
> COACH: 'Doing an audit' is that a task or a goal?
>
> MARK: I see, I suppose it is a task.
>
> COACH: So let's think about these children. In a year's time what do you want to be telling me about them? What will I see if I come into your classroom?
>
> MARK: I want the EAL children to be working in maths with confidence. I want them to be as good in maths as the others.
>
> COACH: Why is this so important to you?
>
> MARK: I believe in equality of opportunity. I came to this school because it had a good reputation for inclusion that is something I believe in.
>
> COACH: So this goal would sit alongside your values?
>
> MARK: Yes, very much so.
>
> COACH: Good, so now let's go back and look at your goal. You said it was to ensure that the EAL pupils made good progress. What is good progress?
>
> MARK: I mean to make the same progress as everyone else, or better even.
>
> COACH: Can you word that into a goal?
>
> MARK: To ensure that the EAL children in my class make average or better progress next year based on their prior attainment.
>
> COACH: I am still not sure what average or better means.
>
> MARK: OK, let's put it this way. To ensure that all EAL pupils maintain or increase their NFER standardised scores over this academic year.

So, finally Mark's goal did measure up in terms of SMART. He had a timeframe, had something he could measure and, most importantly, he had something that he was going to feel proud of, which fitted with his values. One of the reasons

## COACHING AND PERFORMANCE MANAGEMENT

that Mark was able to form a goal so quickly was that he had all the data he needed at the meeting. Mark had done his preparation for the meeting and it made all the difference. The coach very skillfully tapped into the fact that this goal was something that Mark firmly believed in. Mark's goal came out of his fundamental values in education. If he believed in it then he was going to be committed to making it work.

### Exercise

Have a look at some of your school's performance management objectives. If you are a team leader, have a look at your teams, if not, look at your own. Ask yourself these questions.

- Are they SMART?
- Are they really objectives and not actions?
- Are they in tune with your values?
- Are they going to improve the lives of children?
- Are they going to move you forward?
- Do you want to achieve them?
- Do they reflect the school's priorities for development?

After the objectives are set, the member of staff will need to write an action plan. This part of the planning phase is similar to the *Planning for action* stage of the LEAP model. During the writing of this action plan it is important that the member of staff focuses as much on what he/she needs to learn as on what he/she needs to do. It is personal development that the plan is focusing on, not just a list of actions.

The plan needs to cover the following:

- what I need to learn in order to achieve the objectives;
- how I will learn it – reading, observing others, web research, courses;
- what actions need to be taken;
- when it will happen;
- what the success criteria are;
- what support is needed;
- how this links to the school's priorities;
- how the monitoring and evaluation will take place.

> **Exercise**
>
> Look at some of the action plans at school. You may choose one of your action plans related to a PM objective, or maybe a subject leader plan. How do they measure up – is their more of a focus on learning or doing? What do you have to do to change the format? Which bits can you keep and which need to be improved?
>
> **Phase two**
>
> **Monitoring**
>
> Reviewing progress    Giving and receiving feedback    Providing support

## Reviewing progress

It is important that progress against the objectives set is reviewed throughout the year. There are a variety of ways that this can be done and which is chosen will depend on the nature of the evidence that needs collecting. For instance, an objective on pupil progress can be measured by the teacher collecting data generated from ongoing test results. An objective on independent learning could be measured by classroom observation. Classroom observation – or group observation if you are working with a teaching assistant – will generate a lot of useful evidence in terms of monitoring. If an objective concerns leadership skills it may be agreed that evidence is going to be gathered from other staff in the form of questionnaires. As well as evidence collection, there needs to be some sort of interim discussion with the team leader. This will entail giving feedback on the evidence and checking the progress of the action plan.

It is important that the member of staff under review takes responsibility for collecting his/her own data to inform the review.

## Classroom observation

It is much more commonplace these days to walk into a school and find that classroom observation is accepted good practice and operating well. The new Ofsted framework requires that headteachers and team leaders need to have a good grasp of the standards of teaching and learning in their schools, and classroom observation will provide a useful evidence base for that.

Both headteachers and subject leaders now need to have an accurate idea of what the standards of teaching and learning are in their subjects. So there will probably be an established cycle of observations in school. A member of staff needs to be sure why a team leader is carrying out an observation. Is it part of the PM cycle or is it to make a judgement on teaching and learning? Team leaders may not be the only ones carrying out observations in schools, there may also be LA advisers. All the more reason for agreeing with staff on how, when and where classroom observations will take place during the year.

The protocol for classroom observation needs to be set out clearly and there needs to be a distinction made between general classroom observations and those based on performance management objectives.

In the observations relating to PM objectives, the member of staff will have a clear idea of what the focus will be and what the nature of that observation will be. There is a difference between an observation that is going to inform the school's self-evaluation process and an observation on PM objectives. The former will involve a value judgement on the quality of teaching and learning, possibly against Ofsted criteria. The latter will provide factual, developmental feedback based on the focus of the PM objective.

# Giving and receiving feedback – how coaching can help

At best, feedback can be developmental and move staff forward. It can be a hugely rewarding learning experience and have a powerfully positive impact on performance. At worst it can make people defensive and confused. It can demotivate staff and lead to a lack of confidence, which will have a detrimental affect on performance.

Taking a coaching approach to giving feedback will make it a two-way process. The learner will feel a sense of ownership rather than being talked to.

A team member should expect accurate and regular feedback on his/her performance in the workplace. As a leader it is easy to think you are giving feedback when actually you are dropping hints, which go unnoticed. It is tempting to give feedback in terms of general comments for the sake of not wanting to hurt someone. Good honest feedback needs to be regular and as a leader it is important not to wait until something goes wrong to give that vital feedback. There is no need to be afraid of giving feedback. As long as it is direct and based on fact, there should be no problem with anyone receiving it.

COACHING FOR SCHOOLS

> **KEY POINT**
>
> Being a leader is not about having all the answers and scoring points. It is about getting the best from people and coaching them to achieve their best possible performance.

Feedback is important and learning how to do it properly is a skill that needs to be taught. Everyone, not just team leaders, needs to learn these skills. If you are establishing a coaching culture in your school you will be doing peer coaching and the chances are that you will be observing each other. So, everyone needs to learn how to give and receive feedback effectively. Adopting a coaching approach to feedback will give ownership to the person on the receiving end and it will be far more meaningful for them.

Let's look at an example of giving feedback that did not go well.

### Coaching conversation

Ian is head of modern foreign languages at a large suburban secondary school. One of his PM objectives was 'To become more accomplished and confident at speaking to large groups of adults'.

It had been agreed between Ian and his team leader that he would be observed giving a presentation to the prospective GCSE students and their parents.

The following is the feedback discussion that took place after the presentation.

TEAM LEADER: So Ian, well done that went really well.

IAN: Thanks.

TEAM LEADER: Yes I really enjoyed it, how did you feel about it?

IAN: Well, nervous to begin with but overall I am pleased.

TEAM LEADER: The only thing I can pick you up on is, I wonder if they understood it?

IAN: Oh, what do you mean?

TEAM LEADER: Well it's just a hunch. I would not have done it that way and I wondered if it was a bit over their heads. Everything else was fine though apart from it was too complicated.

# COACHING AND PERFORMANCE MANAGEMENT

> IAN: I thought you said it was fine and, anyway, in terms of making it overcomplicated, its hard enough for us to get our heads around the changes, let alone the parents. I was only telling them what was necessary. I was only following the remit given to me by the head. If that's not good enough then I don't know what is.

It is difficult to see what, if any, useful information Ian received in that interview. He did not gain any suggestions for a way forward. Ian's team leader did not use coaching skills in his interview.

All Ian was given were some subjective and judgemental comments. He was given no evidence and nothing that could be acted on. He was not invited to give any detailed self-assessment. Not surprisingly, this led to Ian being upset and defensive.

## KEY POINT

**The two essential elements of effective feedback are making it objective and descriptive.**

Feedback that is given in a coaching style will also invite the learners to comment thoughtfully on their own performance. This kind of feedback will be based on data. The data will be the evidence gathered in the observation and will be delivered to the learner in a straight and uncluttered way. In other words, free of judgements and opinions.

Let's have a look at how Ian's interview could have been handled using a coaching technique.

## Coaching conversation

> TEAM LEADER: Ian, well done.
>
> IAN: Thanks.
>
> TEAM LEADER: I have taken some notes and I have some detailed feedback for you but, before I give you my feedback, I want to gain from you

> some information on how you think it went. What in particular was the most effective part? What could have been improved? What did you learn? Were your objectives achieved? If you could just take a few minutes to fill that in and then we will carry on.
>
> Ian fills in the sheet for five minutes.
>
> TEAM LEADER: OK, so what did those questions throw up for you?
>
> IAN: Overall I was pleased and I think I met my objective. Certainly I was more confident. In terms of the effectiveness of the presentation, well, judging from their questions, I think I may have given too much information. So what I have learned from this is to keep it simpler.
>
> TEAM LEADER: OK, now I have some observations to add to that. First, the way you stood and talked. You stood still and you hardly used notes, which meant you came over as confident. Your tone of voice was steady and convincing because you were not reading it – this had the effect of you coming over as someone who knows what they are talking about. Second, the PowerPoint was effective – you did not read every slide and you avoided using too many special effects. This had the effect of helping the audience to concentrate on what you were saying. Third, about halfway through, you started to use some jargon and acronyms, which people did not understand and I think you lost some of them. This was evident from some of the questions that were asked. Overall, Ian, it was an accomplished presentation in which you came over as confident so your objective is met. Your point for development would be your use of jargon and thinking about the needs of your audience.
>
> IAN: Thanks, that's really useful. I can work on that.

You will notice that every time the team leader made a comment, he backed it up with evidence. When giving feedback it is useful to use language like 'what I noticed was' or 'what I observed was'. It is important that feedback is based on accurate and clear information. That is why the observer needs to take detailed notes. The notes need to be a verbatim account of what actually is happening. In a lesson it is a good idea to keep a log of the time. This would enable you to give comments like: 'I observed that after 25 minutes the children were still sitting on the carpet. The result of this was that a third of them were either talking or wriggling'.

This feedback actually reports on the action and the result of the action. This is so much more effective than just telling someone that his/her introduction was too long.

The team leader also related his feedback to the objectives. Ian was left with a clear idea of what his next steps could be.

Feedback from the self in the form of self-assessment and from others is vital to our learning. People should see themselves as lifelong learners and feedback can form an important part of improving our learning and our performance.

# Barriers to giving feedback

Many people may be reluctant to give feedback. This can be for a variety of reasons, such as:

- 'It's not my job'
- 'It's not my place'
- 'I don't want people to dislike me'
- 'Who am I to judge – I am not perfect'
- 'I don't know how not to upset them'
- 'It will spoil our relationship'
- 'Everyone gets on so well here I don't want to rock the boat'

Not wanting to upset people is a natural feeling. Perhaps it is not in the school's culture to give feedback. If you are building a coaching culture in your school in which people are used to working together in an open and honest way, then giving and receiving feedback should not be a problem.

A common barrier to giving feedback is the reluctance of people to just tell it like it is. Some people shy away from it. It is essential in a PM interview to report back and be specific and direct.

The other aspect of feedback is that it needs to be depersonalised. If you are reporting on what happened in someone's classroom, then you are not saying that they are a 'good' or 'bad' teacher. You are not criticising them as a person. You are simply offering them evidence on what can be improved. You are being constructive.

COACHING FOR SCHOOLS

The key aspects of giving feedback are to:

- make it honest;
- make it factual and direct;
- concentrate on actions and their results;
- give an opportunity for self-review.

## Providing support

The outcome of the monitoring exercises will probably have identified an area of development for the learner. It is all too easy to think that the best way of fulfilling that need is to send someone on a course. However, many heads are now wondering whether this is the most sustainable way of training staff.

We mentioned before about people seeing themselves as lifelong learners. Adults are going to gain more from professional learning if they are involved in planning it. They are going to apply themselves to it if they can see the purpose and they are internally motivated. It is the team leader's job to make sure that there is a climate of learning in the school or department.

Let's look at an example of a section of the monitoring phase interview, and how coaching techniques will provide support.

### Coaching conversation

James is a humanities coordinator in a large urban primary school and he is talking to his team leader.

TEAM LEADER: James, we have got this goal: to make the humanities curriculum more holistic and creative. You have got your action plan. We are now going to look at what support you are going to need to achieve this. First of all, James, what sort of a learner are you?

JAMES: What do you mean?

TEAM LEADER: How do you learn best?

JAMES: Well, when we looked at teaching and learning styles I came over as a reflective learner. I like to have time to mull over things before I do them. I like to work on ideas by myself and then work

# COACHING AND PERFORMANCE MANAGEMENT

> on them with others. The important bit for me, though, is the thinking time alone at the beginning.
>
> TEAM LEADER: OK, now think about your focus. What do you need in the way of training that is going to suit your learning style?
>
> JAMES: I need first of all to work on my ideas. I have done some reading already and I just need time to get my thoughts down.
>
> TEAM LEADER: Good, what next?
>
> JAMES: The next stage would be to involve others, so I could see what the senior leadership team think. I would also like to find out what is going on in the LA so I could take my ideas to the next cluster group meeting. Also the LA adviser might be able to help.
>
> TEAM LEADER: That's great, James. Can I offer a suggestion here?
>
> JAMES: Sure.
>
> TEAM LEADER: I know that somewhere in the LA there is a network-learning group of schools working on this. So it might be a good idea to look on the National College for School Leadership website for more details. OK, now we have some ideas, you need to put them into your action plan with what time is needed and when and we can decide how we can manage that.

You can see straight away how the team leader put the responsibility for writing the action plan on to James. What is also significant is that James was asked to identify his own learning style and build that into his plan.

**Phase three**

**Review**

Self-assessment    Recognition    Professional development needs

The review phase of the PM cycle will be a time for celebrating achievements and recognising what has gone well. Using coaching can add focus for the learner. It is also a time to reflect on what has not been achieved and the explanation for this. As in the first phase, self-assessment plays a key role here. It is important that before the review meeting takes place the member of staff has had a chance to rate his/her own effectiveness over the year. Using coaching-style questions, such as the following, will encourage self-reflection.

- 'What am I most proud of this year?'
- 'What have I learned this year?'
- 'On a scale of one to ten, how do I rate the achievements of my objectives?'
- 'What would have made each one a ten?'
- 'What does this tell me about my development needs for next year?'
- 'Did the action plan work?'

Recognition of achievements has to be the main focus of this meeting. Too many teachers are leaving the profession because they feel undervalued. Of course, good team leaders do not wait until the review meeting to praise their staff. Praise and recognition of a job well done should be ongoing. The PM review meeting, however, provides a more formal opportunity for proper recognition of achievements. It is so easy to swiftly move on to the next thing on the agenda because we are all so conscious of the need for continuous improvement. The relentless pace of change means that we are always moving on to the next thing without savouring those moments of achievement first.

Some people love praise and simply lap it up. Others find receiving praise more difficult. You know yourself when you have said to someone 'I really like your new trousers' they reply 'What, these things? They are not really the ones I wanted. The ones I really wanted were out of stock, now they would have looked better.'

The reason why some people just can't take a compliment could be that they just don't feel worthy enough or perhaps they view it as conceited. In one of the training days I run, one of the activities is for delegates to list ten things that they are good at. There is very rarely anyone who can list that many. People find it very difficult to sing their own praises; it is not in our culture.

## Exercise

Learning to receive feedback is something you may need to work on when developing a coaching culture in your school. You could do the exercise above or you could try the following.

Ask each person to find a partner. Now talk to the partner for two minutes about yourself and your achievements at work, without using one negative word.

Discuss how hard it was to do as an exercise. What does this mean for the person giving feedback?

COACHING AND PERFORMANCE MANAGEMENT

The best way to receive feedback is just to accept it; if it is feedback based on the above guidelines. Then it will be easier to accept.

The following is an example of a review phase meeting where the member of staff is finding it difficult to recognise her achievements. The coach uses coaching questions to get to the heart of the issue.

## Coaching conversation

Susan is a teaching assistant working in a primary school with Year 4 pupils. Her pupil progress objective was: to raise the achievement of my group using the interactive whiteboard.

She is having her Phase three meeting with her team leader having previously carried out her self-assessment of her progress.

TEAM LEADER: Susan, I see from your self-review that you have rated your own progress against this objective as two out of ten. Could you tell me more about this?

SUSAN: Well, as far as I am concerned, only one of the group of six made the required progress, so that is why the score was so low. The objective was not achieved.

TEAM LEADER: Yet you said that you have learned so much this year about the interactive whiteboard. Surely you are pleased about that.

SUSAN: Yes, but that was not the objective, the objective was pupil progress and that was not achieved. I feel very disheartened that I have worked so hard with nothing to show for it.

TEAM LEADER: So what was achieved?

SUSAN: I have raised my confidence in ICT; I know how to use the whiteboard as a tool for learning, whereas before I was scared of it. I just have not managed to raise the achievement of my group using it.

TEAM LEADER: Can you tell me more about that?

SUSAN: Well, the software we had was above them. It was not at the right level. I found that out pretty quickly. So I had to use the whiteboard but make up my own lessons.

TEAM LEADER: What have you learned from this?

> SUSAN: I have learned what works on the interactive whiteboard and what the group needs in terms of software. In fact, the maths coordinator has got it on order. I went to see some being used in another school and I told her about it. I have also learned how to involve the children with the whiteboard and how to excite and motivate them. It is just a shame that in terms of my objective it has not been successful.
>
> TEAM LEADER: What are your views on that objective?
>
> SUSAN: I think that, looking back, we should have written it over two years, not one. The first year should have been to get to know the interactive whiteboard and how to use it with the children. The second year should have been to use it to raise achievement.

Susan had a very valid point about her objective in that it was too far-reaching. I am not suggesting that every time a person's objective is not achieved it is re-written. However, here, it did need to be scaled down. Susan was not able to accept any praise at all because in her own mind her objective was not achieved in full, therefore there was nothing to celebrate.

The interesting point about Susan is that she was able to say straight away what she learned from the experience. One of the key questions for this review meeting should be, 'What have I learned?'

Any part of the objective not met will lead to further professional development needs. Susan had been very proactive and had sought out some best practice in another school. To develop her further in this area, then, she might be asked to trial the new software and then share her ideas and experience with other staff. Clearly a good discussion with Susan at this time, at this stage, will identify some further professional development needs.

We all perform when we feel successful. In the above example, Susan felt that she had failed because her objective had not been met in full. It is important that the team leader is aware of the personal level of skill and confidence when setting and reviewing objectives. Challenges that are too great will instill anxiety and stress. Challenges that are too weak will result in a lack of motivation. Although Susan had not achieved her objective she had learned a great deal that was going to be useful to her. You will notice that Susan's team leader did not talk about success or failure but his assessment was in terms of her learning. We often learn more from our failures or from things that did not go well than from our successes.

## COACHING AND PERFORMANCE MANAGEMENT

> **KEY POINT**
>
> Learning that comes from a situation that does not go well is more likely to become embedded than that from things that go smoothly.

In a school with a coaching culture at its heart, there will be no fear of failure. Success and failure will be viewed as learning experiences. People do not perform well when they are feeling overwrought. Staff will learn more and perform better in an environment where they feel valued and nurtured. So, performance management is not just about measuring performance. It has at its heart developing staff and getting the greatest potential from them – in other words, coaching them.

We know ourselves, from working with children, that they are not receptive to learning when their reptilian brain is in operation. In other words, when they are so stressed their adrenalin is working against them. People learn best when they are relaxed and receptive.

One of the jobs of team leaders is to encourage their staff to be reflective practitioners. During the review phase the member of staff will be asked to reflect on his/her learning and what his/her learning needs will be for the forthcoming year. Staff should also be encouraged to think about how they learn. The following questions may be useful for them.

## Learning questionnaire

I learn best by:

- researching on my own;
- trying things out practically;
- listening to people who have experience;
- watching demonstrations;
- reading about the subject;
- with support one on one;
- watching a video;
- working in a pair.

By identifying their own learning style, staff will begin to see themselves as learners. They can then plot their own learning needs.

The following pro forma will be useful for identifying professional development needs.

| |
|---|
| Current objective<br>Leadership and management<br>Pupil progress<br>Professional development |
| What do I need to learn?<br>Behaviours, skills, strategies |
| How will I learn it?<br>(bearing in mind my learning style) |
| What support do I need? |
| What might the obstacles be to my learning? |

## Chapter summary

Coaching should be at the heart of the performance management system in your school. If you are using the PM system to develop your staff, then you can easily bring coaching into it. Using coaching in PM will have a payoff for staff individually and performance generally.

Each stage of the PM cycle lends itself to a coaching conversation. Giving and receiving feedback can be made non-threatening by using coaching methods.

# Your learning in practice

## The PM cycle

### Planning

- What questions can be asked?
- What can the learner do in preparation for this?
- What can be done in order for the learner to take responsibility?

### Monitoring

- What coaching questions could be asked?
- What self-assessment can the learner do?
- How can we use coaching in giving feedback?

### Review

- What coaching questions could be asked?
- How can we listen to the learner's view of his/her performance?
- How does this session affect future goals?

# 7 Coaching and middle leadership

Middle leadership is becoming an increasingly important area of schools' strategic development. With more emphasis being put on shared and distributed leadership, the middle leader is taking a prominent role.

This chapter is of relevance to anyone who has a curriculum responsibility in a school. It is also aimed at middle leaders who may have a pastoral responsibility or a SENCO role. The other audience for this chapter is any member of staff on the leadership team of a school who has the responsibility for coaching and developing middle leaders.

## This chapter in short

During this chapter we will see what the middle leader's role looks like. We will also examine what skills are now required of the middle leader. We will follow four middle leaders and see how the LEAP coaching framework moves them forward.

We will unpick aspects of leadership and the management of change, which middle leaders may encounter.

## Objectives

When you have completed this chapter you will be able to:

- provide a framework that the middle leader can use to develop;
- take a coaching approach to learning for leadership;
- coach the middle leader through the change agenda;
- provide a self-assessment framework for the middle leader.

## Who are the middle leaders?

Middle leaders are staff members who work in a school with some sort of leadership responsibility who are not the headteachers of the school. Usually, middle leaders will not be on the senior leadership team, but that will depend on circumstances and the size of the school. Often it is the middle leaders in school who have had no leadership training.

Headteachers will have done the NPQH programme. Deputy heads may have followed an LA leadership course, but middle leaders will rarely have had any preparation for their role.

There is more emphasis being put on shared and distributed leadership throughout schools. This means that every teacher within a school who is not an NQT will be a leader in some way. Schools often invest time and resources in training teachers on matters concerning teaching and learning. Very little time is spent on preparation for leadership and that is where coaching comes in.

Middle leaders can be non-subject leaders, year heads, SENCOs or heads of faculty. No matter what their role, they will all be sharing the experience of managing change and leading people.

In some large schools, support staff have some sort of leadership role and are in charge of a team. They will also need leadership training and coaching.

The term 'middle leader' covers a huge variety of staff with a wide range of skills and experience. Let's look at four case studies of middle leaders whom we are going to follow in their journey through middle leadership.

## Case study

Lucinda is an English coordinator and Key Stage 2 team leader in a large inner-city primary school. She is a member of the senior leadership team and has nine years' teaching experience. Maths is her specialist subject, but the English coordinator left and the head asked her to take this on because it was such an important area.

Mike is a mature primary teacher who used to run his own IT company. He is a Year 3/4 teacher in a small, rural primary school. He has just finished his NQT year and the headteacher has asked him to take on the leadership of ICT within the school. There are three teachers in the school for him to lead, including the head who has a 0.2 teaching commitment.

Anne is a SENCO in a large, urban secondary school. She has a team of eight specialist teaching assistants under her leadership. She has 20 years of teaching experience and 2 years of SENCO experience.

Jim is a science department leader in a large suburban secondary school. He has a team of eight teachers and two technicians working in his department. He has a science degree and six years' teaching experience. He is introducing new schemes of work, embedding the Key Stage 3 strategy while the department is being completely refurbished.

---

You can see immediately what a diverse group of people these are. They all have one thing in common. They have to lead growth, development and change in their areas. The idea of the subject leader having a specialist degree in the subject or even an interest is not always true, especially in a primary school where 11 different areas of the curriculum are taught plus the area of SEN. Very often subject leaders are chosen for very pragmatic reasons. Mike was chosen for his technical knowledge. Lucinda was chosen because the area needed someone with strong leadership skills. Ideally a subject leader will have extensive subject knowledge and a passion for that area of learning. However, the truth is that, particularly in primary schools, the subject leader could know no more than the other teachers about the subject. The other aspect of this is that, in a small primary school, a teacher may well lead more than one subject area.

Let's look at some of the issues each of these middle leaders is facing.

COACHING AND MIDDLE LEADERSHIP

# Middle leadership Issues

### Lucinda
- How does she lead an area in which many of the teachers' subject knowledge is greater than hers?
- How does she deal with the fact that, in a high-achieving school, the value added in English is very poor?
- How does she lead very experienced staff who do not see the need for change?

### Mike
- How does he lead other staff, including the head, with one year's teaching experience?
- How does he develop ICT with very limited funds?
- Where does he start with only two full-time staff who have very few ICT skills?
- How does he get ICT on the agenda when it is not on the school's strategic plan?

### Anne
- How does she delegate to a group of teaching assistants?
- How does she build team spirit with a group of part-time staff who are rarely in school at the same time?
- How does she deal with all the SENCO paperwork?
- How does she empower her team members when they lack self-esteem?

### Jim
- How does he manage change with a team of teachers who have a range of experience and varying degrees of enthusiasm for the job?
- How does he make sure that teaching and learning are at the forefront of the agenda when he is also in charge of a building project?
- How does he ensure that his department gets the support it needs from the senior leadership team at such a crucial time?
- How does he keep motivation and morale high in his team?

Although all four of the middle leaders above have very different issues to deal with, they all have the same job to do. Each of the middle leaders needs to be coached by a colleague who has some experience of leadership. Coaching is not the only preparation for leadership. The middle leader also needs to be reading about leadership and maybe attending some training events. However, the effect of any amount of reading or courses will be lost unless regular coaching takes place. It is rather like the apprenticeship model. The middle leader learns by practising and by being coached and supported. In this way, each school can set up its own programme for growing its own leaders – succession planning.

## What is the job of a middle leader?

Very often middle leaders in schools are subject leaders.

The TDA has come up with a national set of standards for subject leaders and SENCOs. It was written in 1998 before many of the current innovations were introduced but still covers many aspects of the role. There are many different aspects to the role and middle leaders' job descriptions will vary from school to school. The aspects of the role I want to concentrate on here are the ones that a coaching framework can help. I see them as the following:

- providing a strategic direction for your subject;
- managing change;
- decisionmaking;
- delegating;
- deploying people and resources;
- holding people accountable;
- evaluating standards in your subject.

You can see that all of the middle leader's issues in our four case studies come under the above headings.

Coaching can help with all of the above aspects of the role. There is an excellent programme for middle leaders called '*Leading from the middle*', run by the National College for School Leadership. This programme is designed so that each middle leader will have a leadership coach in the school. This is a very good model and concentrates on building the leadership capacity of the middle leaders through coaching, training and online learning.

If you are not lucky enough to be on the programme, try to get a senior member of staff to be your coach in this role. Failing that, ask a colleague to pair up with you and find a time when you can coach each other. If neither of those are possibilities you can use the framework in this chapter to self-coach.

Any subject or department will not exist in a vacuum. It will be making a contribution to the school's overall effectiveness. Each subject or department will add to or take away from the success of the school, both in Ofsted terms and in how the school is seen in the community.

However, the subject leader will need to balance his/her own needs and priorities with those of the school and the department.

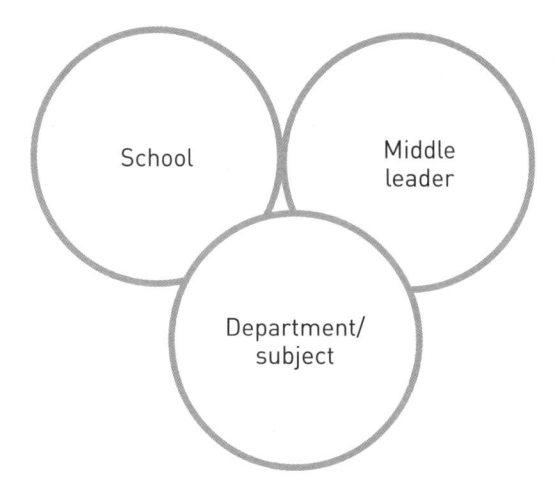

There will always be a conflict of interests for the middle leader, who has to meet the needs of the school, the department or subject and his/her individual needs. The school may have a major thrust for development that is claiming all available resources. Meanwhile, the subject leader may see a huge area of the curriculum that needs developing. The middle leaders themselves could have professional development needs that do not match those of the school. The middle leader will have to perform a delicate balancing act between these three elements of the role.

Some areas of school improvement may be reflected in both the school and the department. Other schools may have agendas that seem removed from the department. In order for the school to work effectively as a whole, the needs of both must be carefully balanced. A good music department can really add value to a school. The school as a whole will value the contribution of that department. It may be good in terms of publicity and the profile of the school. However, it will not exist on its own. Each department needs to reflect the values and overall strategic direction of the school.

## Middle leadership – areas to develop

It would be easy for the middle leader to jump into action, do an audit of strengths and weaknesses in the department and write an action plan, but we are talking about leadership here. If a middle leader concentrates totally on taking action without thinking about what leadership behaviours he/she will need to change, he/she will not develop his/her leadership capacity.

COACHING FOR SCHOOLS

> **KEY POINT**
>
> Using a coaching approach to develop the middle leader will build up leadership skills and lead to deep and sustainable change within the school.

Looking at the four middle leaders in our case studies, they could easily come up with action plans focused on what they need to do. They could continue to focus on action rather than building up their leadership skills. This would lead to continual frustration and limited sustainable development. What they really need to be thinking about and reflecting on is which skills they need to build on themselves as leaders. Then they will to be able to manage the changes ahead successfully.

In order to find out what our four middle leader need to work on, they will need to carry out a self-assessment. Doing an audit of their skills, knowledge and experience is a good starting point for skills development. Ideally, they need to get their colleagues' assessments of them as well, so that they can compare them with their own. So they need to try and find out how their teams see them as well as making their own assessments.

The following sets of questions will highlight their own areas for development. A good idea would be to answer them 'yes' or 'no' on gut instinct and then go back and decide which are the areas of priority.

## Strategic direction

- Do I have a vision for my subject/department?
- Does my plan for the subject/department have clarity and purpose?
- Does my vision reflect the school's?
- Have I shared my vision?
- Do I motivate and inspire staff?

## Managing change

- How do I react to change?
- Have I any change-resisters in my department/school?
- How up to date am I with changes in my area?
- Do I communicate the need for change to staff with clarity and purpose?
- Am I clear about why changes are important?

## Decision making

- How reluctant am I to make decisions?
- Do I consult staff? Too much? Not enough?
- Do I communicate and share my decisions?

## Delegating

- Do I delegate enough or too little?
- Do I delegate with clarity?
- What is my reaction when the tasks I have delegated do not turn out the way I would have wished?
- Do staff I delegate to get the right support from me?

## Deploying people and resources

- Do my budget priorities reflect my strategic goals?
- Is my allocation of money or resources reactive or proactive?
- Are my staff's talents and skills being used properly?
- Are support staff in the right places?

## Holding people accountable

- What are my strategies for dealing with people who do not meet deadlines?
- Do I make my expectations of staff clear?
- Do I follow things up?
- Do I know what I am accountable for and to whom?

## Evaluating standards

- Do I know what the strengths and weaknesses are in the standards for my subject?
- Do I know how to evidence this?
- Do I know the difference between evaluating the standards and reporting on them?
- What is my judgement on the teaching and learning in the subject and how do I communicate that to staff?

The results of this self-analysis should highlight some leadership areas that need developing. Let's return to our four case studies. In them the following themes came through for the middle leaders:

- Lucinda: strategic direction;
- Mike: holding people accountable;
- Anne: delegation;
- Jim: managing change.

All of our four middle leaders are fortunate in that they have someone in school who is willing to coach them on these issues. In Mike's case, because it is such a small school, the cluster has paid a consultant to come in to coach its middle leaders. The other three schools have trained three members of staff in coaching skills. They are going to coach the middle leaders. The coaches working with the four are going to use the LEAP coaching model to work through their issues. The coaching sessions are going to be held once a month.

Using our four case studies, we are going to see how their coaches use the LEAP model to tackle key areas. What will also become apparent is how the coaches focus the middle leaders on leadership skills rather than the action of school improvement.

### KEY POINT

**Middle leaders who are coached in building their leadership skills will contribute to the distributed leadership of the school.**

Our four case studies will illustrate how effective coaching can be in building leadership capacity.

### Case study

Middle leader: Lucinda

Issue: Strategic direction

Name of school: Large inner-city primary

Background: Lucinda's situation is complex. The school is a large primary school in inner-city Nottingham. The school has above-average SEN and EAL pupils. Six years ago the school was in special measures and attainment was ▶

# COACHING AND MIDDLE LEADERSHIP

low. Since then a new head has brought the school's standards up so that it is no longer judged to have serious weaknesses and results have improved. In the last two years the school has had another new head and results attainment at Key Stage 2 is now falling. Two very strong Key Stage 2 teachers have left. The Key Stage 2 department is weak and value added in English for Key Stage 1 to Key Stage 2 is very poor. The problem Lucinda faces is that many of the staff still feel that that school is doing well in comparison to when they were in special measures. The need for improvement is associated, by the staff, with the past. The LA and the community sees it as a school that has improved. The school now has a good reputation. Lucinda's challenge is to provide a strategic direction for English within the school.

---

## Coaching conversation

COACH: Lucinda, you have told me of the difficulties with your subject. What could your subject be like?

LUCINDA: Oh, the potential is for it to be a great subject at the heart of the curriculum.

COACH: Could you tell me more about that?

LUCINDA: It could be lively with all the up-to-date teaching methods. All staff would be committed to the subject. English attainment would be high. We would be well resourced, with English being a very high-profile subject.

COACH: What will I see the pupils and staff doing when that has been attained?

LUCINDA: If you go into any classroom you will find that there are English displays up and the curricular targets are on the walls. You will see enthusiastic pupils in English lessons. The teachers are well informed and using the interactive whiteboards as a learning tool.

I will feel proud that we have achieved success. I will be delighted that the children will be having the best experience they can in the subject.

COACH: Good, you said before that English attainment would be high. Can you tell me what you mean by this?

# COACHING FOR SCHOOLS

LUCINDA: I mean that value added will be high. In other words, their rate of progress between the key stages is good. I mean that they respond well in lessons. I also want them to leave the school with a love of reading and for books.

COACH: It is clear to me that you have a bright vision for your subject. Have you shared that with staff?

LUCINDA: Well they know I have got some new ideas.

COACH: Do they know where it is you are leading them?

LUCINDA: I have said that there need to be some changes, but, no, I suppose I have not actually told them what I want English to look like here.

COACH: Is there something getting in the way of that happening?

LUCINDA: Well I suppose until talking to you I did not really know what I wanted. I had not really thought my vision through. (Silence . . . )

The other thing is that some of the staff have a better subject knowledge than me.

COACH: How does that make you feel?

LUCINDA: I tend to feel nervous and all my confidence goes out of the window. The other problem is that there is a perception that the school is doing really well and there is no need to change anything.

COACH: OK, out of all those challenges that are facing you, which do you want to work on in this session?

LUCINDA: The one about strategic direction. I feel if I had that right then the rest would be easier.

COACH: OK. I am going to give you an exercise to do that will firm up the vision that we have been discussing. It will help you formulate a strategic direction. Once you have that vision you can write a plan, which will be the map for how to get there. You also need to think about how you are going to share that vision with staff.

The format the coach used with Lucinda is as follows.

# COACHING AND MIDDLE LEADERSHIP

| **How to form a vision** |
|---|
| When my vision has been realised, what will my subject be like? |
| What will the teachers and pupils be doing in lessons? |
| What will the pupils attain? |
| What are my goals for English? |
| What are my priorities? |
| How do I share and explain this to colleagues? |

## How did coaching help?

The coach helped Lucinda articulate her vision. By encouraging her to focus on what the pupils and teachers would be doing once her vision was achieved, it made it real for her. Vision is about seeing and we need to be able to visualise the reality of our vision and think about what it is actually going to look like. If you remember, her first response to the question on her vision was 'a great subject at the heart of the curriculum'. That statement lacks meaning and clarity. By asking Lucinda to actually talk about what teachers and pupils would be doing, Lucinda's thoughts became more concrete.

COACHING FOR SCHOOLS

After sharing her vision with staff, the next stage in strategic direction will be to write a plan. There are many different ways of structuring that plan, as shown in the following table. They all need to include goals and the goal-setting techniques used in Chapter 3 can be applied. The plan will also need a timeframe and some costing of resources. A monitoring and evaluation strand of the plan needs to be included. Also there must be something that you can focus on – the end, the success criteria.

| **Action plan** | |
|---|---|
| Area of action to develop my skills | |
| Strengths identified from self-assessment | |
| Areas for leadership development | |
| Where I may get help from | |
| Success criteria | |
| What I will need to work on in terms of my leadership behaviours | |
| Impact on the department | |

COACHING AND MIDDLE LEADERSHIP

Running through the plan needs to be a strand focusing on the leadership skills that the plan is developing. There also needs to be a reference to how the middle leader is going to obtain the help and support that he/she needs.

### Case study

Middle leader: Mike

Issue: Holding people accountable

School: Small, rural primary

Background: Mike is working in a very small, rural primary school with two full-time teachers plus the head who teaches part-time. He has had very little experience of leading and managing school staff. The school is underperforming and English and Maths are the main thrusts of the school's improvement plan. However, the head is very aware that if the school was to undergo an Ofsted inspection, then ICT would not be up to scratch. The head has asked Mike to lead the development of ICT across the curriculum. The two full-time teachers are not that competent in ICT. The school has falling roles and there is very little money available for the development of ICT. The head is delighted with Mike's appointment and she is hoping that he will work wonders on ICT within the school.

Mike and the coach have already discussed the context that Mike is working in and the broad area for coaching. This is the second session. Mike and his coach are at the first stage of the LEAP model.

## Looking at goals

### Coaching conversation

COACH: So Mike, from your self-assessment you came up with holding people accountable as the main area you would like to work on. What is it you would like to achieve in this area?

MIKE: I would like to develop a leadership style that meant I could get people to do things for me on time but maintain a relaxed and friendly manner.

COACH: So what is happening now in relation to getting people to do things?

MIKE: Well, I ask them to do it and then when the time comes they have not done it and they come up with excuses. I get angry and I don't know how to handle them.

COACH: Can you give me an example?

MIKE: Yes, I asked the two teachers to come up with some examples of how they could introduce ICT across the curriculum next term. I gave one teacher the Art and DT and the other one Humanities. They were meant to bring them to the staff meeting last Thursday. They didn't. There was nothing. One said that she had had childcare problems and the other said she had tried and she was not really sure what to do.

COACH: What did you do?

MIKE: Well, what could I do? The head was there and she didn't say anything. It was not really my place.

COACH: How did you feel about that?

MIKE: I felt very angry and let down.

COACH: Did you tell the teachers?

MIKE: No, I can't do that. It is a small school and everyone gets on really well, I can't start getting angry.

COACH: In your last job, you ran your own company employing five people. What did you do when this sort of thing happened?

MIKE: I shouted at them and if it happened again, they got the sack.

COACH: So your previous experience of holding people accountable was to get angry.

MIKE: Yes and that worked. That's the only thing I know. I know that I can't do that here, so what else is there? I know that Rachel has it tough. She is a single mum with very little spare time and lots of childcare issues. The other one, Kate, she seems rushed off her feet all the time.

COACH: You said earlier that you wanted to hold people accountable without getting angry. Can you make a goal out of that which uses more

# COACHING AND MIDDLE LEADERSHIP

> positive language? Tell me what you want to do rather than what you don't want to do.
>
> MIKE: To hold people accountable in an assertive and calm way.
>
> COACH: Good, now let's go back to the task. How did you explain it to them?
>
> MIKE: Yes, well, this could have been one of the problems. It was just tagged on to the end of a staff meeting and I did not have time to explain properly, but I said they could come back to me if they had any problems.
>
> COACH: Anything else you think you may need to do next time?
>
> MIKE: Well, I did not really explain why we were doing it, what it was for. Also I could have given them an example.
>
> COACH: Anything else?
>
> MIKE: No, I don't think so. (Pause...) Well, I suppose that I don't need to get angry. I said I wanted to be assertive. I can just not get drawn into their excuses and just stick to talking about the task I have asked them to do. The trouble is I get angry when they start talking about their excuses because I think, well, if I can manage to do this, then I am sure you can.
>
> COACH: So you want to be assertive?
>
> MIKE: Yes, I want to find a way of leading without getting angry – without losing my temper but so that people will listen.
>
> COACH: Can you word that into a goal?
>
> MIKE: To be a positive, assertive leader.
>
> COACH: Good.

## How did coaching help?

The coach here used silence very well. In the pause, Mike was able to come up with the real issue. This was the fact that he became drawn into people's excuses and got distracted from the task. What also emerged was that he associated holding people accountable with getting cross.

The problem with Mike was that he was being distracted by the staff's excuses, which made him angry. He needed to focus on the task in hand. People will always try to use distraction techniques when they have not done something that you have asked them to do. Like the teacher whom you have arranged to go and observe, who, immediately you walk in the door of the classroom, tries to tell you that she has not had any sleep the night before because she was so worried. These techniques are intended to distract you from the matter in hand. As a leader you need to remain focused on the task that you have asked them to do. The problem is that you stop asking the staff with problems who do not deliver on time because it ends up not being worth the trouble. Consequently, staff who do deliver – irrespective of childcare or other problems – end up getting asked to do things more often.

The other problem for Mike is that one member of staff was not very clear about what needed to be done. Mike had not spent time clarifying the task with the staff. If staff have a clear idea of what they are meant to be doing, there is more of a chance that they will do it.

## Delegating to staff

When asking staff to carry out a task, it is important to remember to:

- clarify the task;
- explain the purpose to them;
- tell them what is in it for them;
- support and encourage them in doing it;
- share your expertise freely;
- set limits and boundaries to the task.

Having established that staff are very clear about what they have to do, they still need to be motivated.

## Motivating staff

Motivating staff is a problem that all leaders will face at some point. The method of motivation Mike used in his previous role was a classic carrot and stick: if you don't do it, you will get the sack. That method was no longer available to him. So, after he has made the task clear and done all of the above, he should try to get staff on his side by motivating them.

People go to work for a variety of reasons. Clearly not many people would work if they did not need the money. Most teachers will be working to pay the bills. Most will also have some sort of vocational blood running through their veins.

# COACHING AND MIDDLE LEADERSHIP

It will be this that helps them get up and come into school every day. Besides the financial rewards, there will be other such reasons why people want to go to work in a school and these are the reasons that Mike needs to appeal to. Reasons for actually doing what Mike has asked fall into a hierarchy:

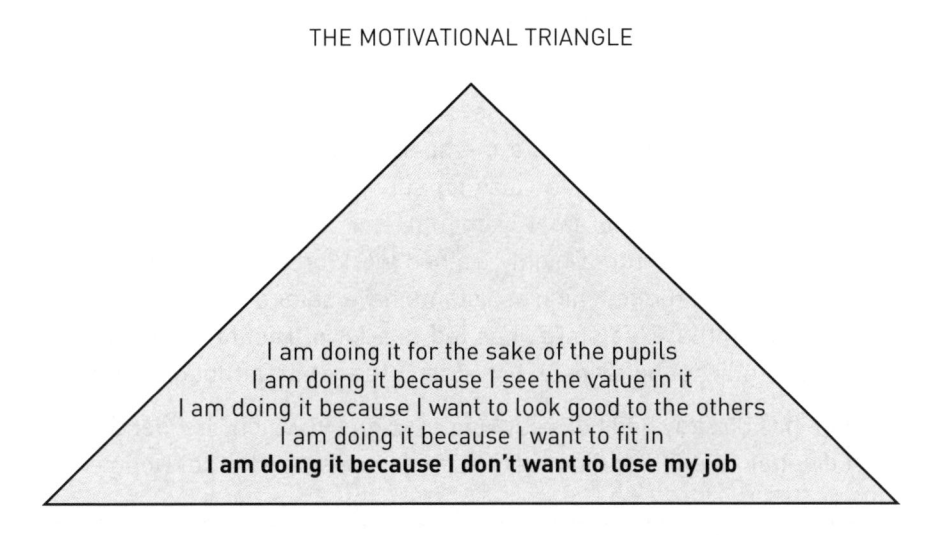

THE MOTIVATIONAL TRIANGLE

I am doing it for the sake of the pupils
I am doing it because I see the value in it
I am doing it because I want to look good to the others
I am doing it because I want to fit in
**I am doing it because I don't want to lose my job**

All of these reasons will motivate staff on some way. The higher up the motivational triangle you go, the more intrinsically focused staff will be and the less attached they will be to extrinsic rewards. So, when tasking something, it is important to aim for the top reasons.

By explaining the task's value to staff and pupils and by 'selling' its benefits, Mike will have a better chance of people carrying it out. Mike needed to make explicit how his task fitted in with his vision for ICT and the values of the whole school.

It was not in Mike's power to sack people and use the carrot and stick method of motivation, so he had to appeal to the higher-level of motivators, such as a person's self-esteem and his/her inner values. Although people may come to work for the money, there are other drivers at work. Factors such as wanting to belong to a team and there being meaning to what you are doing are also important.

COACHING FOR SCHOOLS

## Case study

Middle leader: Anne

Issue: Delegation

School: Large, inner-city secondary

Background: Anne is Special Educational Needs Coordinator in a large, urban secondary school. She is a very experienced teacher and has a superb knowledge of SEN maths. She is a member of the senior leadership team of the school and is successful at making sure that SEN issues are always at the forefront of any school improvements. Her team of teaching assistants has gradually evolved into a highly trained workforce with a wealth of specialist knowledge. All the teaching assistants have gained the higher-level teaching assistant status. This status has led to a bit of friction in the school as they are currently not being paid more than other staff, although that may change.

Anne has already had two coaching sessions in which she identified the areas of delegation and building team sprit as her areas for development.

## Coaching conversation

COACH: OK Anne, what would you like to get out of this session?

ANNE: Well, I would like to review where I am, really. I know we set a goal and I have tried a few things, but I am a bit confused about what to do next and whether or not my goal has been achieved. My goal was to delegate effectively to my team of TAs. I think I have to some degree.

COACH: What does effective delegation look like?

ANNE: It's not having to chase everyone and then redoing the things that they have done because they have not done them properly.

COACH: You have described what it is not. So what is it?

ANNE: That's hard. I don't know... What do you think it is?

COACH: How do you see yourself when this has been achieved?

164

ANNE: Not doing everything myself, being less stressed, not running around after people.

COACH: Is that what is happening now?

ANNE: No, I am stressed, not sleeping, not living up to the demands of the senior leadership team. Yet I have a team of people whom I can't seem to share the work with. So what do you think I should do?

COACH: Anne, I can see you're overwrought so I am going to give you some advice about delegation. Is that all right?

ANNE: It's fine.

COACH: Effective delegation is when you empower someone else to carry out a task. Proper delegation can really enhance team spirit because it shows that you are trusting staff and giving them responsibility.

ANNE: You used the word 'empower'. You mean that by delegating you can develop their skills?

COACH: Yes, absolutely.

ANNE: I see, I had never thought of it that way. I just thought of it as a way of offloading tasks to make my life easier. I felt guilty about that.

COACH: So yes, it will develop staff and be empowering to them to think that they are trusted and valued. Shall we think about ways in which you could put this into practice?

ANNE: I am still not sure.

COACH: What's getting in the way of this?

ANNE: At the moment I am the leader of the team. I get paid more and they all look to me to run things, I have the power and I do the most work. If I delegate what happens to that power, are we all the same or what?

COACH: So you are saying that because you are the leader you have to do everything otherwise you will lose your power?

ANNE: Mm, this is all really interesting. I think what I am saying is that I am afraid that if everyone is empowered and doing the things that I used to do, it will make me less of a leader. I will have less power and they will have more and who will be in charge, them or me?

> COACH: If you have a team that is empowered, who will be making the decisions, setting the strategic direction, allocating tasks, deploying resources, motivating staff?
>
> ANNE: Yes, I will and I suppose that is what leadership is all about. That is what I am paid for, not doing everything myself. Yes I see.
>
> COACH: By delegating, you can increase people's job satisfaction, develop their skills and give them a sense of purpose in their work.
>
> ANNE: I understand now what delegation is. How do I do it?

### How did coaching help?

Anne was tired and at the end of her tether during this session. The coach obviously realised this and deemed it necessary to offer some advice. There are times during coaching when this is appropriate. Of course the coach is going to be there as someone with experience and it would be ridiculous to ignore this. The coach's intervention actually led Anne to have more of an insight into what was going on in her head and what was stopping her delegating.

Delegating to someone requires that you coach him/her. When you are delegating a task, you need to offer support and advice to the person you have delegated to. If you view delegating as developing someone, then you have built success in to begin with. Anne's staff are not used to being delegated to, therefore she needs to start with something easy. She also needs to be very clear on the task and set time limits. She needs to make clear whether the person is required to report to her at intervals on the progress of the task or just required to show her the end result. She also needs to make clear how much autonomy the person has over the accomplishment of the task. There is nothing worse than a leader who delegates and then asks repeatedly how the task is going. You need to be able to allow your staff to do the best possible job that they can. Often it will not turn out in the way you had imagined and it is important for leaders to let that go. People have their own ideas and they bring their own originality to the task. There is nothing wrong with this as long as Anne has made sure from the beginning how much leeway there is. Often delegation goes wrong because all these aspects are not made clear at the beginning. When you next delegate a task, try to check what you have done against these points.

- Have I made clear what the task involves?
- Have I made the timeframe clear and is that realistic?

- Has the person the skills to carry out the task?
- Have I made clear the level of information I need about how the task is progressing?
- Have I given enough support, encouragement and feedback?
- Have I begun with an easy task and then increased the difficulty?
- Will the task enhance the individual's skills?

### Exercise

Look at your action plan for your subject or department. Which of the actions have you delegated? If the answer is none, how are you going to develop your delegation skills? If you *have* delegated, have you done that with empowerment? Check out your delegation with the above checklist.

What do you now need to do?

### Case study

Middle leader: Jim, head of science

Issue: Managing change

School: Large suburban secondary

Background: Jim is teaching in a popular secondary school in a leafy suburb of Bristol. The department has good results and is well regarded by the rest of the school. The labs were very out of date and refurbishment is long overdue. The school has looked at teaching and learning and this has meant various changes in the curriculum for the department to take on board. Jim is leading his department through a time of change at many levels. On a purely physical level, there is the refurbishment of the department, which means that classes are being constantly moved and equipment is being stored in different places. On a curriculum level, he is introducing new schemes of work and new teaching methods. Some members of his department are relishing this challenge, others are resisting it.

Jim has already had one coaching session and this is the second, one month later.

# COACHING FOR SCHOOLS

## Coaching conversation

COACH: Now Jim, what was the goal we decided on last time?

JIM: To enable the department to understand the changes that were going to happen and accept them.

COACH: So how has that gone?

JIM: Pretty good. They do all understand what is going to happen. Most of them are excited, but there are a couple who are not happy and they are the influential teachers who are listened to by the younger ones.

COACH: OK, so is that what you would like to focus on today?

JIM: Yes.

COACH: So what is the goal?

JIM: To use my leadership skills to manage the resistance to change in my department.

COACH: So how would you like it to be?

JIM: This is a difficult time for all of us, I don't deny that, but, I would like all members of the department to be looking at the advantages that these changes will bring and be enthusiastic about them.

COACH: What does enthusiasm look like?

JIM: It looks like just not being resistant to every little thing that is changing here. All the time I am met with a wall of resistance to everything. There is nothing that gets by the two I am thinking about, that does not get moaned about or picked to pieces. They are making everything more difficult. It really is pulling the rest of us down and I can see the younger members of staff being dragged down with them. Things are difficult for all of us. What is the point in them making it worse?

COACH: What have you tried already with them?

JIM: I have argued with them about the benefits the changes will bring. I have told them time and time again about the benefits. Every time they start, I try to counter what they are saying with reasons why this is going to be so good. I can't let them really let rip or it will have a worse effect on morale.

COACH: You have already got them to understand that this change is going to happen no matter what?

JIM: Yes, that was my goal from last time and that was hard enough, this now seems impossible.

COACH: OK, getting them to accept the change was dealing with their intellect. Now you are meeting with resistance, you are dealing with their feelings.

JIM: What do you mean?

COACH: They know the change is going to happen – they have given up denying that – but now they are stressed and worried about it. This always happens to people. They always go through this cycle with change. The important thing here is to listen to the resistance.

JIM: No, I can't do that. That means they have won. I have to resist their resistance.

COACH: What happens if you continue to do that?

JIM: Well, one of us will get worn out and give up – and it won't be me.

COACH: If they give up, does that mean morale will be any higher, will you have won them over?

JIM: In the long term, no, they will still rumble on, but what is the alternative to meeting their resistance with mine and biting back?

COACH: What is the alternative to resisting it?

JIM: Letting it happen?

COACH: Yes, and, more than that, listening to it. Giving it a platform rather than resisting it.

JIM: That's risky. What if everyone agrees and joins in?

COACH: What happens when you don't meet resistance with resistance, you just let it happen?

JIM: I suppose the person resisting probably gets fed up.

COACH: Yes. If you give your resistors a platform, they will feel listened to. The reason why they are resisting at the moment is because they are feeling stressed and worried. You are not listening to their feelings or even allowing them a platform to express them. They need to know that you, as their leader, understand their feelings. The more you refuse to listen, the louder they will get.

### How did coaching help?

Jim was getting worn down by trying to meet the resistance to change in his department with his own arguments. Actually he was trying to block that resistance. The coach enabled Jim to realise that if he gave staff the chance to express themselves and be listened to, then the resistance would probably dissipate.

Jim tried to match the resistance he experienced with his own reluctance to hear it. He should have welcomed it.

Resistance –
greet it
name it
move on.

By greeting it instead of meeting it, you will ensure that you are acknowledging the fears and feelings of the resistor. By naming it, you are flushing it into the open and giving the resistor time and space. By moving on, you are allowing the resistor to develop without being labelled and the resistance is forgotten.

In managing change, a team leader needs to be aware of the cycle that people go through.

The model below is adapted from Scott and Jaffe's *Managing Organizational Change: Leading your team through transition* (Crisp Publications, 1989), which they explored the psychological effects of change.

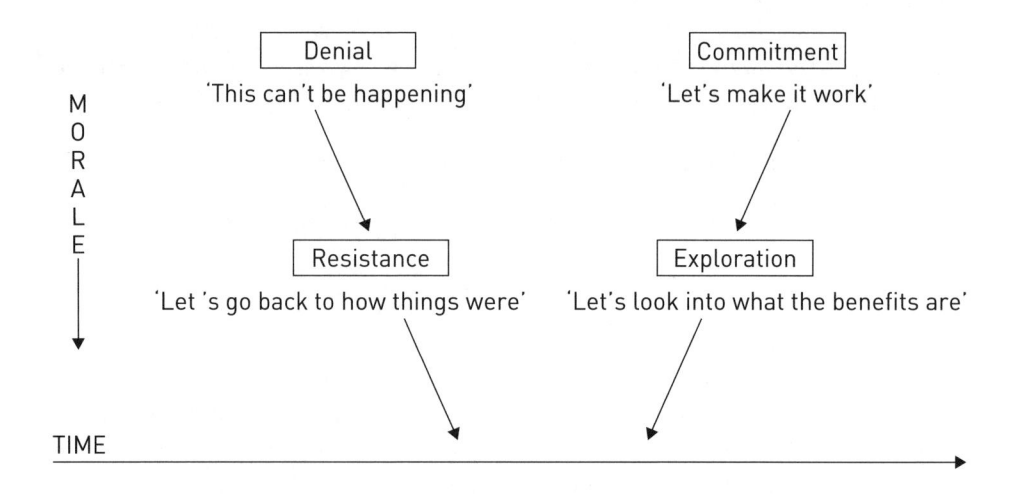

```
                    ┌─────────┐                        ┌────────────┐
                    │ Denial  │                        │ Commitment │
                    └─────────┘                        └────────────┘
              'This can't be happening'            'Let's make it work'
   M
   O
   R
   A
   L
   E
                           ┌────────────┐              ┌─────────────┐
                           │ Resistance │              │ Exploration │
                           └────────────┘              └─────────────┘
                 'Let's go back to how things were'   'Let's look into what the benefits are'


   TIME ──────────────────────────────────────────────────────────────────▶
```

# COACHING AND MIDDLE LEADERSHIP

Some of Jim's team were in the Resistance phase of the cycle and, unless he gave them time and listened to their worries, they would not be able to move on to Exploration and Commitment.

The role of the middle leader in this cycle is to be aware of and facilitate every stage.

The middle leader needs to do the following as the team members move through the cycle.

- **Denial** – be assertive and get the team to understand that the change will happen.
- **Resistance** – deal with people's feelings, listen to them.
- **Exploration** – try to capture the creative energy and have discussions on people's ideas.
- **Commitment** – sustain the change, get staff the resources and support that they need.

### KEY POINT

**If the middle leader accepts that these phases in introducing change are inevitable, then they will be well equipped to steer the team through them. It is the job of the coach to enable the middle leader to recognise them and move though them.**

### Exercise

Think of a change that has been introduced in your school recently. Can you plot the phases of change that people have gone through against the Scott and Jaffe model? What did people say and do at various stages? How did the team leader act? If you were coaching the team leader, what would you have said?

COACHING FOR SCHOOLS

## Chapter summary

Each of our middle leaders faced different challenges. They were able to draw out their learning about leadership from those challenges with the help of their coaches.

Coaching the middle leaders in schools can lead to deep and sustainable change within their teams. The middle leaders need to be trained and coached in leadership skills.

The development of the middle leaders took place because they had goals linked to leadership rather than purely action planning relating to their departments.

# 8 Coaching and strategic development

## This chapter in short

This chapter will apply a coaching framework to schools' strategic planning. It will examine how a school can set goals and achieve them. The crucial importance of taking time to reflect and evaluate will be illustrated. In particular, it will emphasise the importance of planning for leadership development. It will look at three case studies of schools to see how they have improved the strategic development process by using coaching techniques.

## Objectives

When you have completed this chapter you will be able to:

- show how a coaching approach to strategic planning can lead to sustainable change;
- show how the school community can be involved in the strategic development process;
- explore the process of goal-setting in relation to strategic planning.

# Strategic planning in schools

Strategic planning in schools usually takes the form of writing a school improvement plan (SIP). All schools are involved in a pattern of school development planning, usually on a cycle of anything between one and five years. The SIP will outline the major projects and themes that the school will be working on. The content of these plans will be determined by a variety of factors: post-Ofsted action points, self-evaluation form findings, national initiatives and local issues or SATs results. The way that schools tackle their development strategy can determine their success and the sustainability of that success. The process that a school goes through to write the SIP will be as important as the plan itself.

During the year, issues other than what is on the SIP will crop up and have to be dealt with. Both these new issues and the themes of the SIP can be tackled within a coaching framework.

To improve the strategic development process, a series of coaching questions can be used to define the action areas. By going through this process schools will be able to decide what it is they actually need to work on. In other words, define the area for development and focus.

At each stage of the planning process it is the following coaching-style questions that will raise the level of the strategic planning and make it more sustainable.

The five stages of the strategic planning process are:

- Stage one – Vision, aims and values
- Stage two – Goal-setting
- Stage three – Action planning
- Stage four – Implementation/monitoring
- Stage five – Reflection/evaluation.

Any school needs to build reflection and review in to the strategic planning process. If all you are doing is planning action and carrying it out, you will never have a chance to actually establish what the school is there for. The following questions, used in the five stages of school improvement planning, will embed the action plan into the heart of the school.

## Stage one – Vision, aims and values

- What are we here for?
- What does this school value?

- What will this school not compromise on, no matter what?
- What sort of school do we want for our pupils?
- What is this community of staff and pupils aiming for?

**Stage two – Goal-setting**

- Where do we want this school to be in five years' time?
- What will that look like?
- What will the pupils be experiencing in five years' time?
- What will the effect on pupils be of attaining these goals?
- How will we know when we have achieved them?
- Do our goals reflect our vision and values?

**Stage three – Action planning**

- What actions need to happen in order to achieve these goals?
- Who is going to lead the actions?
- Who is going to carry out the actions?
- Over what period of time will they happen and when?
- What resources are needed?
- What training is needed?
- What coaching is needed?

**Stage four – Implementation/monitoring**

- Are these goals still appropriate?
- What are the factors affecting them?
- Have the needs of the pupils changed?
- Are the goals still going to benefit the pupils?
- Is this still something we want for our pupils?
- How are we collecting the evidence that we have achieved our goals?

**Stage five – Reflection/evaluation**

- What has the effect on pupils been of achieving these goals?
- Have we used our resources in a cost-effective way?

- What have the results of our actions been?
- How have we measured them?

> **KEY POINT**
>
> **By asking the coaching questions at each stage, the school is raising the awareness of staff and building into the cycle the constant reflection that is often missing.**

A school would not have to go through this whole process every year. Stage one of the cycle – the vision, aims and values – would only be redone when necessary. However, it is worth revisiting vision and values whenever the school may have a new headteacher or new staff. Vision and values do not just look after themselves. It is easy to put the vision in the school prospectus and then forget about it. Buying into the school's vision and values should be part of the induction process for every new member of staff and every new governor. Many schools start the academic year by re-examining their vision. It is good practice to remind staff of what they are actually at the school for, before getting bogged down with the planning and aspects of writing the SIP.

Stages two and three tend to happen with a flurry of activity at the beginning of the academic year. It is then easy to get preoccupied with the implementation stages as the year rolls on. By asking the coaching questions above, the school will be checking out the validity of the actions taken.

The two stages of the strategic planning cycle I would like to examine closely are stage two, goal-setting, and stage five, reflection/evaluation.

## Stage two – Goal-setting

Everyone in a school has dreams about what they would like the school to be like. The pupils, staff and parents will all have ideas and aspirations for the school. The difference between a goal and a dream is that a goal has a positive commitment and is backed up by daily action. Dreams and ideas are fine, but, if action does not follow, then they achieve nothing. A school will need dreams and ideas but, behind those, there need to be clear aims and objectives backed up by a plan to channel the school's resources and energy. Let's look at a case study to illustrate this point.

# COACHING AND STRATEGIC DEVELOPMENT

> **Case study**
>
> Nailswell School is a small primary school situated in the rural outskirts of Bristol. Two-thirds of the school was housed in Portakabins, which were pretty shabby. The school had dreamed for years of having brick-built classrooms added on to the existing building. Everyone who visited the school remarked on its superb ethos but also said it was a shame about the buildings. The governors and headteacher had been in dispute with the LA for years about the fact that the Portakabins were technically condemned and did not meet health and safety requirements. Every year the LA promised to replace them, but some other building catastrophe came up elsewhere and the funds were reallocated. Their dream of classrooms seemed to become further out of their reach year by year. A permanent new member of the governing body joined who changed that. He was a professional fundraiser for a charity. He started asking questions that made the school reflect on its previous actions. One such question was, 'What is the most important goal in the school currently?' They replied, 'For the whole school to be housed in permanent buildings.' He continued, 'What is your plan to achieve this?' They replied, 'To ask the LA every year because it is their responsibility.' He asked, 'What else have you tried?' The governors had to admit that they had not tried anything else, maintaining that the funding of the new buildings was the LA's responsibility and they looked to them for provision.
>
> The school had become locked into battle with the LA and did not have a proper strategy. The new governor set to work on this. Within three years the governor had put together a plan and added interim goals to their long-term goal. With the plan, the governors secured funding from various sources and the classrooms were built. The LA met a small one-quarter of the cost. The new governor made the dream into a goal by giving it commitment and taking action.

By taking a coaching approach to your goal-setting you will be able to define and clarify your school's dreams into goals.

Setting goals needs time and each goal needs to be re-examined in steps. This system of goal-setting has four steps, during which goals are defined and clarified.

The process of goal-setting assumes that the school has already set its vision and values. Obviously, stage one of the strategic planning cycle needs to have happened before goal-setting can take place. Otherwise the goals would be without the direction or belief to back them up.

So, let's assume that your school's vision and values are agreed and you are ready to set your goals.

## Step one

This needs to be carried out with all the staff and representatives of the whole school community. It is best to divide the groups up so that there is a mixture of all stakeholders in the group. This first step is the one in which people can be allowed to dream. It is important at this stage to be imaginative.

*The task: write down on paper everything you want the school to be in the future. Think about what you want for the staff, the children, the parents and the community. Let the ideas flow.*

It is important at this stage to accept everything and make sure everyone has an equal voice. The various groups can share their ideas and see what they have in common.

## Step two

After getting together the ideas from each group, they need to be collated into one list. A smaller group may better carry out the second step, with all stakeholders represented.

The aim of this stage is to align the list of goals with the values of the school.

*The task: for every item on your list, ask the following questions.*

- *Why do we want this?*
- *Which of the school's values does this reflect?*
- *What will the benefit be to pupils?*

The goals that cannot stand up to the above scrutiny need to be discarded. Only the goals that are relevant to the school and reflect its aims and values should remain. This process should have narrowed the list down.

## Step three

At this stage it is important to look at the kinds of activities that go on in a school. Some of the dreams and aspirations of the school community may not

# COACHING AND STRATEGIC DEVELOPMENT

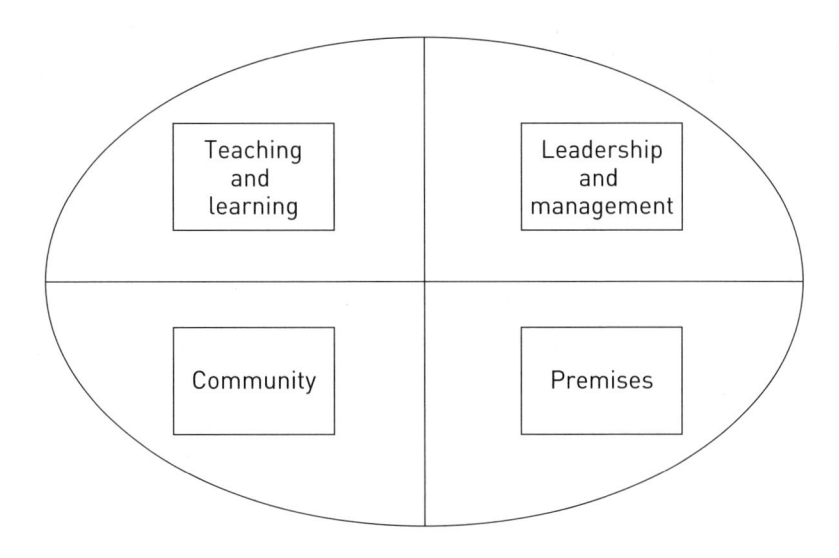

```
         ┌─────────────┐      ┌─────────────┐
         │  Teaching   │      │ Leadership  │
         │     and     │      │     and     │
         │  learning   │      │ management  │
         └─────────────┘      └─────────────┘

         ┌─────────────┐      ┌─────────────┐
         │  Community  │      │  Premises   │
         └─────────────┘      └─────────────┘
```

necessarily come into the school's remit. I have defined the development of the school under the headings given in the figure.

Each of the school's goals can be matched up to one of the four headings in the figure.

This stage is best illustrated by looking at a case study.

## Case study

Name of school: Southern Park Primary

Context: Large, urban school in Birmingham

The headteacher had been in post for a year. During her first year she had followed the SIP format of the previous head. The school had gone through a period of instability with an acting head for a year. There had been a 50 per cent turnover of staff and the head now wanted to establish the commitment of the whole school community to the strategic planning process. The school buildings were in a poor state of repair and the attainment of Key Stages 1 and 2 were historically below LA averages. The next few years would be a challenging time for the school as it was about to be merged with the adjoining nursery and become a children's centre.

The head had used an outside facilitator to take the school through stages one and two of the goal-setting process. She used a smaller group of representatives to come up with stage three. They split the goals up, assigning them to the four headings, and came up with the following list.

### Southern Park Primary's goals

*Teaching and learning*

- All teaching to be good or better.
- All pupils to be actively and independently engaged in their own learning and development.
- All pupils to make satisfactory or better progress in all subjects.
- Pupil attainment will reach national average of similar schools.

*Leadership and management*

- To be graded one on the LA's categorisation system.
- All subject leaders will be working efficiently and proactively in their roles.
- To have a strong and established senior leadership team and governing body shaping the strategic direction of the school.
- To ensure that the school's financial planning underpins its goals and aspirations.

*Premises*

- To establish a safe and aesthetic learning environment throughout the school.
- To ensure that all resources are of high quality, relevant and stored effectively.
- To develop and use the outside school environment to enrich the curriculum.

*Community*

- To place the school at the heart of the community it serves.
- To ensure that the provision of the 'Every child matters' agenda is facilitated within the school site and reflects the needs of the children at Southern Park.
- To ensure that the children of Southern Park become responsible and caring members of the community.

**Step four**

This stage will involve the prioritisation of the goals. It is important to decide how many goals it is feasible to have on a strategic plan. It is sometimes tempting to want to work on too much at any one time. The number of goals will depend on the size of school or department.

*The task: put your goals in order of priority. Decide how many goals it is practical to have and select that number from your priority list.*

The goals on the list may be short- or long-term goals. The goals that will take more than a year are the ones that will require an action plan and, therefore will need to be part of the SIP.

Decide which of your goals are short-, medium- and long-term. Finally, are your goals SMART? (Specific, Measurable, Achievable, Realistic, Timeframed.) Finally, are all the goals expressed in positive language?

You are now ready to go on to the action-planning stage of the school development cycle.

The other stage in the strategic planning cycle that benefits directly from a coaching framework is stage 5.

# Stage five – Reflection/evaluation

You will notice that I have combined the evaluation stage with the reflection stage. The reasoning behind this is that, while the actions of the SIP are being carried out, the school needs to reflect and ask questions constantly. With Ofsted's new framework focusing more on self-evaluation, many schools are now in a cycle of self-evaluation and are used to using the results of that process to inform the school's SIP, taking an analytical approach to school action planning.

If reflection and evaluation are combined, then there is no danger of a school getting bogged down in the doing stage of the plan and not stepping back to just check out whether or not the actions are still appropriate and right for the pupils. It is easy to get stuck in that 'plan, do' cycle of improvement, to get bogged down in the planning and implementation stages of the cycle and never really fully reflect on what has been achieved.

# COACHING FOR SCHOOLS

The old adage is, 'If you do what you have always done you will get what you have always got'. So, schools that are constantly looking for new methods of teaching without evaluating the old ones will always repeat their mistakes and get the same results. It is easy for a school to get stuck in provisions and planning without focusing on outcomes first. Using a coaching approach will highlight this.

For instance, let's take Severnmouth Primary School, based on a council estate in Harlow. The headteacher is discussing this year's focus for development with his coach.

## Coaching conversation

COACH: So Andrew, what are the main issues facing the school in the next academic year?

HEAD: Well, it is the same old thing really, attainment at Key Stage 2 in maths and English. Attainment is well below the average for our group of schools.

COACH: How do you know that is the issue?

HEAD: Because that is what the SAT results tell us and we have to do something about it. I already have the LA on my back.

COACH: What have you tried already?

HEAD: Oh, you name it. We first have identified the underachievers. Then we managed to get the resources to fund teaching assistants working with them in small intervention groups. We have run all the intervention groups, Early Literacy Strategy (ELS), Additional Literacy Strategy (ALS), Springboard. We have also tried taking groups out to have small group work to reinforce skills with ICT. We really have tried everything.

COACH: What have the results been?

HEAD: SATs remain the same, no improvement.

COACH: What does that tell you?

HEAD: That we have not found the right teaching methods in the small groups. We need to find the right programme for them. We have spent ages identifying the right pupils to take out. It is just a matter of finding out what works with them.

# COACHING AND STRATEGIC DEVELOPMENT

> COACH: So what do you need to do now?
>
> HEAD: I need to do some research from our cluster schools and the rest of the LA to see what teaching strategies they are using in their intervention groups.
>
> COACH: What do you think the research will show you?
>
> HEAD: That we need to use some different strategies in our groups. We know the kids we need to work with, we just need to keep on taking them out of class with the teaching assistants, but using some different strategies with them.
>
> COACH: So you plan to carry on with taking the groups out?
>
> HEAD: Yes, definitely.
>
> COACH: What evidence do you have that having intervention groups works?
>
> HEAD: Mm, good question. (Silence . . . ) Well, having a small group is bound to be better. Isn't it?
>
> COACH: How do you know?
>
> HEAD: Maybe that's something we may need to look into. Well I suppose research shows that the higher the teacher–pupil ratio the better . . . I have always thought that these children need more individual attention. It's just a feeling of wanting to do the best for them. I suppose we haven't really researched it.

## How did coaching help?

The coach asked Andrew the 64-thousand-dollar question: *'What evidence do you have that having intervention groups works?'* Andrew was planning to continue with the same strategy without even evaluating it from last time. He was about to identify the pupils and set the groups up for another year without evaluating whether having intervention groups in his school was an effective strategy to use or not.

Resources in school are always very limited and Andrew was willing to put a lot of his spare funding into staffing those groups without knowing if, as a strategy, taking small groups out of the classroom was successful.

Andrew and his team had put a lot of time and effort into identifying the target pupils for the groups and planning how they were going to work. It is easy to see why the school was very keen to make them work after investing so much time in them.

Andrew's school had become so bogged down in the planning and the doing that they forgot to reflect and evaluate. They had become preoccupied with the management of the groups. The consequence of this was that none had stepped outside of the present and reflected on the success of the groups.

Objectivity in evaluation is difficult when a lot of time, effort and faith have been put into projects. However, it is necessary to distance oneself from the situation and properly reflect and evaluate.

Here are the questions that Andrew's team should have been asking themselves.

- What impact have the intervention groups had on the learning of the pupils in them?
- What impact have the intervention groups had on the rest of the class?
- What impact have the intervention groups had on the self-esteem and attitudes to learning of the pupils in them?
- How cost-effective have the groups been?
- What is the value added of having them, in terms of the children's learning?
- What are the outcomes of having these groups?

Coaching helped Andrew find out what the real issue was. His real issue was not 'How to find out which teaching strategy works in the intervention groups', it was 'Are intervention groups effective?' Coaching lifted Andrew out of the humdrum of providing for the intervention groups and encouraged him to reflect on the rationale for the groups.

Reflecting and evaluating are real stages of the strategic development process. They are perhaps the most important. Andrew's school had not reflected. The provision of the intervention groups had not produced the pupil outcomes required. The school focused on the provision of the groups rather then the required outcomes for pupils, which was to improve their attainment. All their planning had been focused on how they were going to deliver teaching to the groups, based on the assumption that groups would guarantee a rise in attainment.

### KEY POINT

**The focus of any strategic development needs to be on pupil outcomes rather than provision.**

# COACHING AND STRATEGIC DEVELOPMENT

Andrew's school had made the assumption that a high teacher–pupil ratio and taking groups out of the classroom would work. The evidence that this strategy would work was not based on evidence and research.

## Coaching on specific issues concerning strategic development

We have seen how a coaching approach can help with the whole cycle of school improvement planning. Let's now look at two case studies where a headteacher has used a coaching style with her staff to solve some strategic development issues.

### Case study

A 100-place nursery school in inner-city Leicester is facing changes that will alter the status of the nursery. The staff are uneasy about the changes, as they fear there are going to be redundancies. The nursery is known locally for its excellent practice and used to have Beacon status. A new head has taken up her post. The staff are not sure what to expect of the new head and are very proud of their record-keeping system. This system was noted in the last Ofsted inspection and highlighted as a strength of the school, which was praised.

The new head found that the school's record keeping was not as she thought at first. She identified that the children's records were not providing the useful information that the nursery needs.

The children's records were very time-consuming to produce and were taking many staff hours to prepare. The records are something they have been praised for in the past, although staff do acknowledge they take far too much time, especially in the light of Workforce Reform. The records were not in the spirit of reducing the amount of time staff spend on administration tasks.

The baseline for the records was established on the pre-school visit when the parents answered a number of questions on what their children could do. The head felt that this did not create the right atmosphere for the visit, the purpose of which is to get to know the child and the parents and begin a positive relationship.

The problem with the information about the children was that it was anecdotal and parents wanted to present the children in the best possible light. As ▶

a result, these baseline indicators were often inflated by parents anxious to show the children as capable to the nursery staff.

Because of this, when it came to measuring the children's progress a term later, the records showed that the pupil's progress had deteriorated because the initial record was inaccurate.

Subsequent updating of the records was very time-consuming and the teachers had not put the record in a form that would be useful to a reception teacher, as it did not relate to the Foundation Stage Early Learning Goals.

When faced with this problem, the head, who was newly in post, approached it in a coaching way. She capitalised on the staff's dissatisfaction with the amount of time the records took and asked them the following questions.

- What do we want from our children's records?
- What is their purpose?
- Who are they for?
- What do we want to achieve by keeping them?
- Does the present system reflect our school's aims, vision and values?
- How do the records benefit pupils?

By working through this process, the staff were able to come to an agreement that the record-keeping system they had in place did not fulfil their needs. The staff had been fully involved in this process and they wanted to make the next step. They had been encouraged to define the problem themselves and come up with an answer. If the head had imposed a solution, she would probably have met with resistance. Instead, she trusted that the staff had their own answers to the problem within them. The staff were the experts on their context and situation; they were the ones who best knew what they needed from their record-keeping system. They also knew what would be manageable in their situation.

The head then asked them to set goals defining what a useful system of record-keeping in a nursery setting looked like and they were then able to use this as a starting point to devise their own. They then moved into the action-planning stage of the development of this issue.

Clearly the staff were more committed to making the new system work because a coaching approach had been used than if the head had imposed a new system on them.

COACHING AND STRATEGIC DEVELOPMENT

## How did coaching help?

The staff had lost sight of the original purpose of the records. They had invested a lot of time into building them up and getting the process right. They had never actually asked themselves if the resulting records were appropriate or useful. It took the objective eye of the new head to see the situation as it was. By going back to the goals of the record-keeping system and establishing what the benefit to pupils was, the head got them back on track.

> **KEY POINT**
>
> **By using a coaching approach to goal-setting with the staff, the head identified the real issue.**

The second case study looks at a much broader issue.

In this case study, the head uses a coaching approach to tackle a strategic development issue.

> **Case study**
>
> The head at an inner-city Bristol primary school with 600 pupils had a specific issue that she wanted to explore and so employed a coach for a limited number of sessions. The following account is the result of three discreet one-hour coaching sessions.
>
> The head was concerned about the new teachers' pay and conditions structure that was aimed at rewarding excellent teachers and taking away management points and making them leadership points. There was a firm drive to raise standards in the school and she wanted a new leadership structure that would support the raising of standards and be in line with the new pay and conditions.
>
> She wanted to be creative with the leadership structure in the school and find one that involved all staff as team members with team leaders. Traditionally the teams had been based on the division between upper and lower school and she felt that this was not working. There were innovative and creative members of staff whom she wanted to involve in the leadership structure.
>
> The head had many ideas, but she lacked a structure to build on. By using a coaching framework, she was able to come up with a starting point.

The questions the coach asked her are in bold.

## The coaching session

**So what do you want the leadership structure to do at the school?**

- To support the raising of standards in the four core subjects in the school.
- To involve all staff in the long-term strategic development of the school.
- To establish a shared leadership structure.
- To create a flatter leadership framework.
- To encourage staff to work more collaboratively on leadership issues.
- To reflect the new pay and conditions regulations.

**What is the goal here?**

- To create a leadership team at the school that reflects the needs of the school and moves it forward.

**Which key areas are at the heart of the development of the school?**

The key areas are:

- technology;
- communication;
- inclusion.

**Could you justify why those areas are important?**

- *Technology*

    This is pivotal to improving standards in teaching and learning because the hardware we have got is really inspiring our children, but we need to integrate it into the curriculum far more. We have made a massive investment in ICT and we now need the use of it to embed in the curriculum.

    ICT is a cross-curricular subject, having impacts on the core areas that we need to raise standards in.

    Monitoring, assessing and evaluating ICT are crucial parts of this area, as we need to know what we are doing well and where our development areas are.

    We need to look at ICT in the infants to see what sort of competency our pupils are coming to us with on entry to school.

- *Communication*

    At this school we believe that parents, as empowered and effective partners, will help us work towards raising standards in the attainment of pupils.

# COACHING AND STRATEGIC DEVELOPMENT

Literacy across the curriculum is pivotal to our development, it is one of our key areas of development.

The wider community is important in terms of involving the whole community in the development of the school; we have to communicate successfully with them. We need to use our facilities to help parents learn and boost their self-esteem.

- *Inclusion*

  We have lots of intervention programmes aimed at raising standards.

  We have gifted and talented challenge groups in place.

  We need to challenge children who are just below average.

  Assessment for learning is a strand that needs to be woven into the leadership responsibilities.

After the head had justified why these three areas where so important to the school, she established that she wanted three teams based on these areas. Each team would have a team leader who would be asked a series of coaching questions to establish what was needed from a team leader. In this way the following person specification for team leaders was developed.

### Personal qualities and what we will expect of team leaders

What about the people? How are they more than a subject leader in school?

- They look beyond the school.
- They will have a good knowledge of the whole curriculum.
- They need to have a clear vision.
- They need to relate all objectives back to teaching and learning.
- They need to be an excellent classroom practitioner in the subject.
- They need to know how to conduct a classroom observation.

What personal qualities will they need?

- Good interpersonal skills.
- Someone who listens.
- Business skills.
- Financial knowledge.
- Excellent subject knowledge.

What's your role as headteacher in this?

- To have an overview of whole teams.
- To challenge teams and ask questions.
- To take risks.
- To make teams accountable.
- To encourage teams to self-assess their effectiveness.

### How did coaching help?

The head was able to come up with a strategy to move the staffing structure forwards. She had an idea of what she wanted, but nothing further than that. The coaching process helped to clearly define her goals and what her team leaders would look like. From here she was able to write the job descriptions and interview for the posts.

## Coaching for sustainable change

You will notice in all the case studies that nowhere was anyone told what to do by the coach. The headteacher of the nursery school could well have known what the answer to the record-keeping system was. Indeed, she could have brought one from her old school and simply enforced it on the staff. She used coaching because she wanted sustainable change and development in her school.

When using coaching in schools, with everyone doing similar jobs, it can be very tempting to tell someone rather than coach them. The coach will have some knowledge of the job involved and may be tempted to offer solutions. There is a place for telling, but not in a coaching session and not where coaching techniques are being used.

> **KEY POINT**
>
> Telling, like expressing sympathy, engenders a dependency culture, which is not what coaching is about. Instead, we are looking at building sustainable teams who are capable of absorbing changes.

In a school with a coaching culture, everyone is constantly learning and coaching each other.

Teams of staff who are used to being coached and who are coaching each other will be resilient to the constant barrage of new legislation and innovation that hits schools from all directions.

A school that is teaching coaching skills to the staff will not only be ensuring its own future development but also developing a far better place to work. Imagine a school where everyone is trained to show empathy, listen to learn, be non-judgemental and establish rapport. Coaching skills are essentially communication skills, which can be applied to many areas of life. By investing in coaching, a school is investing in the future of its staff and the institution. Schools are dynamic institutions that need to be robust in order to grow and develop. Teaching staff the skills of coaching will ensure that they are equipped to deal with change and have the capacity to do so.

## Coaching and leadership development

Every school has a section on its SIP that covers the curriculum – this will normally come under teaching and learning. Few schools will have a section on leadership and management. By far the most important part of the plan will be that concerning leadership, for it is the pivotal feature of any school. What is the point in having 24 different action plans if there is no one in the school with the skills to lead these projects forward? Leaders in school can make a difference. We have already looked at subject and department leadership and seen what a difference a highly skilled team can make. However, this has to be planned for. Teachers need to be taught how to lead; it is not something people are born with.

There are many leadership programmes available to schools and they can buy in leadership training from a variety of providers. The National College of School Leadership has a leadership strategy with a programme for leaders at all levels. What schools need to do is look at the leadership capacity within the school and predict what its needs will be and who it needs to develop.

The school's strategy for developing leadership should not begin and end with someone going on a course. Regular coaching sessions are needed to build on learning. Learning about leadership is best embedded when it goes hand in hand with a series of coaching sessions. A large school may decide to appoint a number of leadership coaches who would coach emerging leaders within the school. A smaller school may appoint a leadership coach across the cluster.

COACHING FOR SCHOOLS

Each member should have a pro forma that outlines who his/her coach is and how his/her leadership development will be tackled, as shown in the following table.

| |
|---|
| Name:<br>Position in school: |
| Leadership responsibilities: |
| Leadership coach: |
| Coaching sessions – one per term: |
| Leadership training: |
| Leadership areas to develop: |
| Name of coach: |
| Date of review: |

# COACHING AND STRATEGIC DEVELOPMENT

> **Chapter summary**
>
> This chapter has provided a framework that builds coaching into the strategic development process in schools. We have seen how goals can be re-examined to ensure that they reflect the school's values. The three case studies have shown how coaching has uncovered what the real issues in strategic planning are.

## Learning review

Look at your SIP. Take your goals through the five-step process. Do they need refining? What are your training needs now with regard to strategic planning? How are you going to tackle building leadership capacity in your school?

# 9 Coaching the team

## This chapter in short

This chapter considers the function of a team, describes how coaching can make teams work more effectively together and defines the key features of the 'learning team'. Case studies of two teams are analysed to discover what is moving them forward and what is holding them back. Finally this chapter will show how the LEAP model can move teams forward.

## Objectives

When you have completed this chapter you will be able to:

- define what makes a team a learning team;
- apply a coaching approach to team development;
- explore how the team members balance the needs of the team with their own individual needs;
- show how the team can be coached to deliver a task while reflecting on and improving its own performance.

## What are teams and what do they do?

A team is a group of people who work together. The purpose of a team is to work together so that the sum of that work is greater than that of the separate individuals.

Teams may be formed for different reasons. For instance, a working party in a school may have been formed for one specific reason to carry out one specific task. An example of this is the school change team. This working party or team will have been formed to see how best to implement workforce reform within school. It will include representatives from all the people involved in the reforms (teachers, leaders and support staff) and its purpose will be to establish the reforms and then monitor them.

Another example is the leadership team of a large secondary school. This will include the headteacher and senior leaders drawn from all sectors of the school. It may meet weekly and has many functions. There are always several tasks and projects that it will be involved in. This team is well established but its members will come and go as people change roles. Occasionally staff members will be invited to join because the project they are running has a high profile in the school.

Other teams will be comprised of staff performing the same job within the school. For instance the teaching assistants of a school may form a team, as may the lunchtime supervisors or the administrative staff. Some teams may have a designated leader, others will not. Some teams will have structured meetings with agendas, others will be more loosely organised and just come together when they are needed.

In a large school, a primary function of a team is to ensure that each part of the school knows what is going on and has an equal stake in the decision-making process. Clearly, making all the decisions that affect the school is too much for one person and does not make for a very democratic organisation, so giving teams responsibilities is a way of making the leadership of the school more collaborative.

Spreading the workload is a good reason for using teams. Utilising the expertise and drawing on the skills of a wide range of people is another reason for forming a team. Some teams will have real decision-making powers. Others will be there to disseminate information but in reality have very little power. The amount of power the team has will depend on how flat or hierarchical the leadership structure within the school is. What goes on within a team will depend on what its function is.

Within a school there will be many different teams and any one member of staff could be a member of several teams. A person could be a leader in one team and a team member in another. Switching between roles can be difficult and present challenges both to the team and the individual. The number of people making up a team will vary as well. In a small school, the leadership team may consist of two people – the head and the senior teacher. In a large secondary school, the leadership team of the school could consist of six people. Probably the largest and most diverse team in a school is the governing body, which can consist of up to 25 members.

All teams are made up of very different individuals. Their reasons and motives for being part of that team will vary. Some people will be there because they have to; it is just part of their job description. Others will be on the team because membership of the team can do something for them. They may perceive that being a part of that team will be good professional development for them. Others may become team members to drive their own agendas forward. Some members of a team may be there because they want their voice or the voice of the organisation to which they belong to be heard. With the 'Every Child Matters' agenda embedding more in schools, teams are being formed that include professionals from outside agencies and organisations. A school representative may find him-/herself a member of a team with people from local charities, the health service and social services. A team like this may be formed to launch a particular project in which each group has a stake. The reasons for belonging to the team will affect the behaviour of the individual. The team member will exist in two guises – that of the team member and that of the individual. There will sometimes be a conflict of interest between the two that can affect team performance.

So there are various teams, both within the school and that it may be involved in in the community and they are all different, but what do they all have in common?

- They will all be working together for the good of the pupils.
- They will meet regularly.
- They will represent different groups or stakeholders in the school.
- They will all have a shared purpose.
- They will all be made up of a diverse mixture of people.

Some teams work effectively, others don't. A team coach can improve the performance of a team. Some teams may decide that they need an outside person to come and observe them and act as a coach in order to help them work together more effectively. In other teams, the team leader may coach the team so it performs better. If the team is to be coached, it must first decide what it aspires to and what makes an effective team.

## Exercise

Name at least three teams in your school. Think about their composition and list the members. What are the motives of the team members? Why are they there? What are they expecting from the team and how does this affect their behaviour? Think about the teams that you belong to. Do you act differently in them? How do your different roles within the teams affect your behaviour?

# The characteristics of an effective team

Before discussing how to make the team more effective, we must first decide what an effective team looks like. It is important that the characteristics of an effective team are established so that its performance can be measured. For a moment, consider one of the teams you are in. Imagine that it is working superbly well. What would I notice if I were to come into a meeting of this team? What would I see, hear and experience? The following case study explores some of these questions.

## Case study

Name of school: Grove Primary

Phase: Primary

Size: 250 pupils on roll

Catchment: Inner city

Background: Karen is a new headteacher of a primary school that has just amalgamated what were separate nursery, infant and junior schools. The leadership team contains representatives from the nursery, infant and junior schools. Each school fought the amalgamation fiercely. The school had been identified by the LA as likely to be judged to have serious weaknesses if Ofsted inspected it. Improving the quality of teaching and learning was high on Karen's agenda when she arrived, while the rest of the team did not share her sense of urgency. She is going through the LEAP cycle with her coach and is presently in the *Looking at goals* stage.

**L**ooking at goals

**E**xploring reality

**A**nalysing possibilities

**P**lanning action

She is talking to her coach about how she would like her leadership team to be in the future in order to be able to set the appropriate goals for them.

## Coaching conversation

COACH: So Karen, if I were to join a meeting of your leadership team in a year's time, what would you like me to be hearing, seeing and experiencing?

KAREN: You didn't say feeling and that is the most important one for me.

COACH: OK.

KAREN: I want you to be feeling excitement. Yes, really it has got to be as strong as that. I want it to be tangible. I want you to see that people feel pride in belonging to such a good team. I want you to hear laughter and I want you to see people with a sense of purpose, working hard and fully committed. I want you to be able to see people working together for the good of the school, people wanting to make a real difference to pupils.

COACH: Can you explain a bit about what working together looks like?

KAREN: Yes. It means having common objectives and, if that means sometimes letting go of what you personally want, then so be it. It means working together for the greater good, for the benefit of the pupils of the whole school, not just one department. It means viewing the school as one entity.

COACH: So everyone is working towards common goals.

KAREN: Yes and it is more than that; I would like them all to leave their egos and their histories at the door.

COACH: What do you mean?

> KAREN: I mean that I want them to all trust each other. I want them to be able to almost know what the others will *do* next because they are all familiar with what each other's strengths are and are able to use them. I want them to be able to speak freely and express their opinions. I want everyone to feel that they have an equal part to play and that they are all valued.

Karen presents a very graphic account of her ideal team. To summarise her account and build on it, we can list some of the characteristics of an effective team:

- open communication;
- trust and openness;
- common goals;
- agreed ground rules;
- knowing and utilising each other's strengths;
- knowing each other's weaknesses and compensating for them;
- a shared purpose.

Karen also said that she wanted them to 'leave their egos and their histories at the door'. In other words, she wanted the people in the team to be prepared to discard their personal agendas for the good of the team. She is asking team members to put the team's common goals and purpose above their own.

Karen's coach continued to examine the reality of what the team was like in the next session; in other words, the *Exploring reality* stage of the LEAP model.

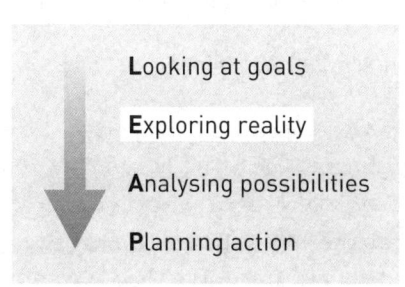

**L**ooking at goals

**E**xploring reality

**A**nalysing possibilities

**P**lanning action

## Coaching conversation

> COACH: Karen, you have presented a very vivid picture of how you would *like* your leadership team to be. Can you describe it as it is *now*?

KAREN: Well, how long have you got? There are people there who did not want the amalgamation to go forward and are stuck there. It is almost as if they cannot accept that it has happened. They said it wouldn't work and they are going to make sure that it is not going to.

COACH: They are being obstructive.

KAREN: That's it. Then there are two members of staff vying for my attention who are competing with each other. They went for the deputy's job and didn't get it. There is also someone who wants to be leading the show and is treating the team as an exercise in showing that he is ready for a leadership post.

The most disappointing thing for me is that everything I try to do is impeded by these old rivalries and because they have scores to settle.

COACH: Can you give me an example?

KAREN: Yes. The school day.

COACH: Go on...

KAREN: The infants are having too many breaks. They have a break in the morning to have their fruit, then they have assembly and then they have their playtime. This covers about an hour when absolutely no teaching and learning is going on. It is crazy. If Ofsted came in next week – which they could well do – we would be slammed for it.

COACH: So what should be happening?

KAREN: The most obvious thing to change is to do away with the 'fruit break' and have them eat their fruit in the playground. The thing is that this has been suggested and the early years staff don't like it. They say the needs of the very young children in the school are not being considered and this is just what they were afraid would happen when we amalgamated.

Karen described much interference that was getting in the way of her team performing effectively. The coach moved on to unpick ways in which these interferences could be worked on. The barriers that stopped the team working together, were:

- rivalry;
- lack of trust;
- no common goals;
- pursuit of personal agendas;
- wanting to look good in front of the team;
- not wanting to make mistakes;
- fixed positions.

Karen's team has provided us with an example of two extremes. The most important issue is how is she going to move her team from where it is now to where she wants it to be? The answer lies in coaching the team.

# What is team coaching?

Team coaching is different from individual coaching, but the principles are the same and the LEAP model can still be used. It can be approached in four different ways.

### 1. The team coach

A team can appoint a coach who is outside of the team to work alongside it. This coach observes, asks questions and is very much a facilitator. The coach tries to get the team members to reflect on their behaviours as a team and will sometimes comment on how individuals are working. The team coach moves the team forward on its agreed goals.

### 2. The team leader as coach

In this scenario, the team leader also coaches the team. This role is very challenging for the team leader. The leader has to develop a degree of objectivity when working with the team. The team leader must develop some independance and distance him-/herself from the team. The leader has to sacrifice what influence he/she may have on the team for the sake of coaching them. The team leader must take a long-term view in this case. He/she must see the development of the team as more important than achieving the task that has been set.

## 3. The team that adopts a coaching style

This team will be highly effective. It will have got to the point where all issues are discussed openly and there is a free flow of honest dialogue. This team will put its own effectiveness above personal success. It will probably have started off having a team coach and now have become self-sufficient.

## 4. The team leader is coached

The team leader will make the topic of his/her coaching sessions the development of the team. As we saw earlier, Karen was talking to her coach about how to make the team more effective. All the goals that are worked on with the coach will relate to the team's development. The coach will work with the team leader, prompting him/her to find his/her own solutions for making the team work more effectively.

Someone who is appointed as a coach for a team will be working to ultimately do him-/herself out of a job. The coach will be working to make the team self-sufficient and work effectively without him/her. This coach will be external and it can be useful that he/she is are not familiar with all the ins and outs of the personal histories of the team members. He/she can remain neutral.

# The stages of team coaching

The stages that a team coach will work through with the team are taken from the LEAP model:

**L**ooking at goals

**E**xploring reality

**A**nalysing possibilities

**P**lanning action

### Stage one – *Looking at goals*

At this stage, the coach is helping the team to define its purpose. The coach will need to lead the team to discover what it is trying to achieve and why. The team needs to think about what it is working towards. Questions such as,

'What would happen if we were not here?' and 'How can we make the most significant contribution to the running of the school?' significant need to be asked.

The coach will ask the team to continually self-evaluate its progress against its purpose. It needs to define its goals, not in terms of tasks it is carrying out but in terms of how members work together. The coach will encourage the team members to reflect on their processes of working together rather then the content of what they are doing.

## Stage two – *Exploring the reality*

The team coach will at this stage need to use team members' observational skills. The coach will act a facilitator and observe the team, asking questions such as, 'What is actually happening here?', 'How inclusive are you being?', 'How challenging are you being?', 'Is everyone being heard?'

After gathering evidence, the coach will report back to the team, giving objective feedback. This feedback could be based on the criteria that the team has previously identified as being those of a highly effective team.

At this stage the team coach will help the team to identify the barriers that are preventing it from performing well. The team coach must maintain his/her impartiality as the feedback he/she needs to give the team could be quite challenging. At this stage conflict will need to be brought to the surface in order for the team to progress.

These barriers could be down to personality factors or lack of skill on the part of the team members. Whatever the barriers, the team coach will need to facilitate an open dialogue that explores these issues openly.

## Stage three – *Analysing possibilities*

The team coach will be asking the team members to go through all the possibilities they can think of to achieve their goals. At this stage the team will be thinking divergently and everyone's contribution needs to be recorded. The team coach will need to facilitate a rich and fruitful discussion.

Roles within the team could be discussed at this point. The team coach will be asking questions such as, 'How will you know when that has happened?' and 'What does open communication look like'.

## Stage four – *Planning for action*

This is where the team will decide on its plan to become a learning team. Out of all the options available from stage three, it will choose which ones it will work

# COACHING FOR SCHOOLS

on. The team coach's job at this point is to pin the members down to a timeframe and decide on success criteria against which to judge their action points. This stage will deal with the practicalities of how the team is going to develop its capacity to become a highly effective learning team.

> **Exercise**
>
> Consider yourself a team coach or team leader or member who is going to coach the team.
>
> What are the similarities between team coaching and individual coaching?
>
> What are the differences in the processes?
>
> What particular skills will you need to be a team coach?

## How do teams work?

When you are coaching a team, you need to understand how it is working. Teams are formed and then go through four stages of team development. The best-known model to describe this process was originally developed by Bruce Tuckman, see Figure 9.1.

The reason that this four-stage model is presented as a circular diagram is that at any time the team can revert back to the previous stages. This can happen when a new member joins the team and changes the dynamic. It can also happen when the team takes on a particularly challenging task. It is the job of

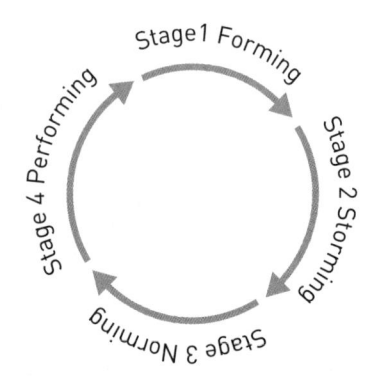

**Figure 9.1** Developmental sequence in small groups

the coach to make sure the team progresses through the stages and does not revert to becoming less effective.

Let us now look at the stages in the model and see how the coach can move the team forward at any of these stages. Whether the leader is acting as coach or there is an outside coach, it is important to be aware of the stages. There are certain behaviours you will see and hear at every stage. Each stage will demand something different of the coach or leader as coach, so we need to examine each stage in detail.

## Stage 1 – Forming

The team at this early stage is anxious to please. It will want to show its leader or coach just how well its members can work together. There will be no one who wants to rock the boat by starting an argument. There will be pressure on everyone in the team to conform and gel together quickly. Everyone in the team will want to belong and know what his/her place is in the team. All teams will start in this place. Even if some of them know each other already they will act in this way at the start.

The team members will want roles and will model what they think are acceptable team behaviours. However their behaviour is pretence and masks what is really going on. There is a lot that is not being said at this stage.

For instance, there may be one person who is dominating the team and, although nothing is said, the others feel unhappy about it. Dissatisfaction is felt but not voiced until the meeting is over.

What the coach will see:

- enthusiasm;
- people outwardly showing that they are listening: nodding, smiling;
- people leaning forward – open body language;
- people anxious to move on and finish the task;
- people wanting to be right;
- people wanting acceptance of their ideas.

What the coach will hear:

- agreement – 'that's a good idea';
- acceptance – 'no, that's fine, I don't want to hold us up, you go ahead';
- manners – 'I am sorry, I did not mean to interrupt';
- peace and stability – 'we all get on well here'.

What the coach should do:

- discourage the dependence on the coach or team leader – the team will be looking to him/her to provide clarification and direction;
- discourage the team from trying to please the coach or leader;
- distance him-/herself from the team;
- ask questions that encourage each team member to reflect on the part he/she is playing;
- ask the team to rate its performance out of ten and, for anything less than a ten, ask 'What would it take to make it a ten?'

## Stage 2 – Storming

It is during this phase that the personality of each team member will come to the fore. People become more relaxed with each other and less well behaved. In the previous stage, the team members were concerned to act as one in order to finish the task. Team members will now try to persuade others to be on their side and see their version of events. At this point there will be conflict. The team members may feel that they are not making any progress. The task may need to be abandoned and put to one side while the team concentrates on how it is working. There may be some frustration expressed because the team members are disappointed after having made a seemingly good start in Stage 1. They may feel that they are going backwards. It is at this point that they could question the competence of the team leader or coach. They will be seeking guidance.

What the coach will see:

- individuals asserting themselves;
- conflict;
- people acting defensively;
- reactive body language;
- some disengagement;
- confusion.

What the coach will hear:

- disagreement – 'that is not true';
- people stating their own opinions and points of view – 'I must disagree with that';
- a reluctance to acknowledge what is going on – 'we are just trying to get to know each other';
- impatience – 'we just don't seem to be making any progress'.

What the coach should do:

- give firm guidance to the team without being defensive;
- give the team factual, evidence-based feedback;
- encourage the team to name the conflict that is happening;
- manage the conflict carefully;
- discourage the team from wanting to go back to the first stage and repair conflict without resolving it.

**Stage 3 – Norming**

This stage is difficult for the team. It has come out of the 'honeymoon' period of Stage 1 and has to get to a phase in which members' individual differences have been aired. They now need to settle some of their disagreements for the sake of the team. They need to decide how much of themselves they should hold on to and how much they can let go of, in order for the team to move forwards. At the beginning of this stage their differences are unresolved. However, as they begin to think about the goals, they will start to trust each other and a balance begins to emerge.

What the coach will see:

- the members acknowledging their differences;
- the members beginning to see each other's points of view;
- the development of trust;
- a growing rapport between team members;
- some real and deep listening developing between team members.

What the coach will hear:

- the members trying to understand each other – 'I want to know where you are coming from on this';
- the members beginning to listen to each other – 'can we make sure everyone is heard here';
- the members beginning to realise each other's strengths – 'Alec had a good idea about that – let's hear it again'.

What the coach should do:

- use his or her facilitation skills to encourage the team members to listen to each other in order for them to learn about each other;
- encourage them to see each other's points of view;
- challenge the team to focus on common goals.

## Stage 4 – Performing

In this stage the team functions as a group of people working together towards achieving a common task. This can be a special time for the team. It is quieter and are free of personal conflict and agendas. As a team the members become free to concentrate on the task. The members will enjoy working together and they trust each other. The team can make decisions quickly and is focused on its common goals. The team members begin to think as a group and do not encourage non-team members to join.

What the coach will see:

- creativity and imagination;
- people prepared to take risks;
- the task driving the team;
- a problem-solving approach being adopted;
- enjoyment in working together;
- a positive working atmosphere.

What the coach will hear:

- more quiet acceptance of each other;
- ideas being exchanged;
- relaxed humour;
- acceptance of each other.

What the coach should do:

- make him-/herself redundant;
- challenge the team to take a problem-solving approach;
- encourage creativity;
- challenge the team's thinking.

## How to use this model

This model is a useful tool because it allows the coach to plot the development of the team. The coach will know that different questions need to be asked of the team at different stages of the team's development. This model can be used in a variety of ways. The coach may decide it would be beneficial to share it with the team. It can help members understand that what they are going through is part of a normal cycle that they will work through.

In time the team members may begin to recognise the stages themselves. This will encourage them to be more reflective themselves and become truly a 'learning team'.

Although a team may have reached the performing stage, it will not necessarily remain there. There will be leavers and joiners who will affect the team's performance. If this happens, the coach can help the team to move through the stages more swiftly. Indeed, if the team has reached the stage where members are using a coaching approach, they will be able to do this themselves.

### Exercise

Think of the teams you have belonged to and identify at which stage of the Forming, Storming, Norming and Performing cycle they were. Try to think of a time when the team was at the other different stages and what it looked like. The following questions may help you in identifying the stage:

1. Are you so eager to get on with the task that there is very little time spent on the planning of it?
2. Are team members afraid to ask each other for help?
3. Do you have fixed roles and procedures for working?
4. Do you have shared goals that are clearly stated and regularly revised?
5. Does your team have a shared sense of responsibility for the team's success or failure?
6. Do you have fun as a team?
7. Is there a sense at the end of meetings that people want to spend more time together?
8. Do you avoid conflict and want everyone to feel comfortable?
9. Are you challenged as a team member?
10. Do you get a lot of work done?

Now that you have answered these questions, try to identify which stage of development your team is at. Use the pro forma overleaf to note down your evidence.

### Stage 1 – Forming

How do you know?

What do you see and hear as a team member?

What do you feel as part of that team?

How does that team approach a task?

### Stage 2 – Storming

How do you know?

What do you see and hear as a team member?

What do you feel as part of that team?

How does that team approach a task?

### Stage 3 – Norming

How do you know?

What do you see and hear as a team member?

What do you feel as part of that team?

How does that team approach a task?

### Stage 4 – Performing

How do you know?

What do you see and hear as a team member?

What do you feel as part of that team?

How does that team approach a task?

## Balancing the needs of the team

A team is made up of individuals. In a highly effective team, a 'learning team', the individuals will be working together as one unit. The individual team members have not forgotten their identity, they have taken on a team personna in which the needs of the team will come first. In any team there is always a balance between the individuals' and the team's needs. We saw that, in the example

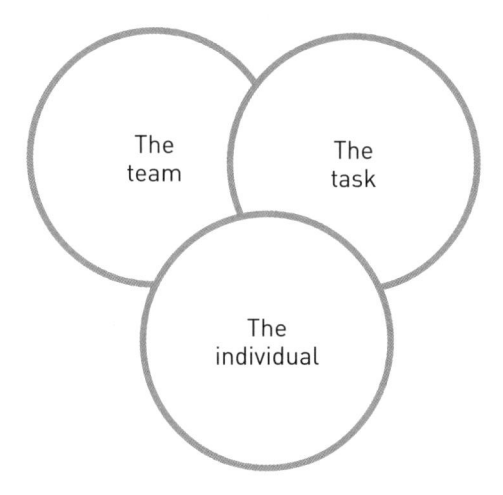

**Figure 9.2** Working with teams
*Source*: John Adair *The Concise Adair on Team Building and Motivation* (Thorogood, 2004)

of Karen's school, the individuals had points that they wanted to make about the amalgamation. At the stage that the team was at they were not prepared to put those to one side and think of the needs of the whole team.

The other balancing act that goes on in a team is balancing the needs of the team and the individuals with the task. Obviously the team has set tasks to achieve. All teams will be under the pressure of time to make decisions and produce results. However, there will be a need for team members to work effectively and this demands that everyone has his/her say.

John Adair has devised a useful model (see Figure 9.2) for demonstrating the three different but overlapping areas of need in a team.

This simple model can be used to analyse what is going on when a team is working together. It provides a framework for us to look at team behaviour and motivations. The team leader or coach will need to be aware of the delicate balance between the three circles. They each represent an area of need for the members of the team: that relating to the team, that relating to the task and that relating to themselves. Sometimes there will be a conflict between the three circles. At any one time the balance of the three circles will vary. They are all interdependent and the coach has to bear all three in mind constantly. The most effective teamwork will take place in the part where all three circles overlap. In other words, the 'learning team' will have the three areas of need carefully balanced so that the task is achieved, the team is developed and the individual has a learning experience from being a part of the team.

COACHING FOR SCHOOLS

## The three circles

*The team*

The team will need to have effective communication, clear goals, defined roles and mutual support.

*The task*

The task will need systems and organisation. It will also need focused working and a clear timeframe.

*The individual*

The needs of the individual will vary enormously. Each person will have a different learning style. Each person will behave within the team in a different way according to his/her personal style. Each person will have a different motivation for being a team member.

This model is a useful tool for the team coach or leader. When giving the team feedback on how it is performing, you can ask each individual to initial where in each circle they thought that they were operating and ask them to explain. This is a good way of encouraging team members to reflect on how they are working together and developing as a team.

It is useful for team members to see how they move from one area of the circles to another as the task and their approach to it varies. The model also provides a non-threatening way for team members to give each other feedback on their behaviours, both collectively and individually.

In order to illustrate the use of this model, let's look at our second case study in the shape of Wickfield School.

## Case study

Name of school: Wickfield Community School

Phase: Secondary

Size: 1,200 pupils on roll

Catchment: Large, rural town with some light industry and farms. The school serves four outlying villages

Background: The school is popular and successful. Recently there had been some anecdotal feedback from the community and governors that local employers were dissatisfied with the competence of the last few cohorts of school leavers. The school decided to conduct a survey of local businesses. This showed that, although school leavers achieved good passes at GCSE and A level, they often lacked the basic skills and competences to do a job.

The school was also anxious to respond to the personalised learning agenda and had wanted to move towards a competency-based curriculum. They decided to construct a 14–19 pathway curriculum with the introduction of Business Training and Educational Council (BTEC) First Diplomas as an alternative to the traditional route. The objective was that students would be able to follow the route that best suited their needs.

A team of heads of department had been set up to try and plan this curriculum and it was not making any progress. As a result the headteacher had asked an external coach to come and coach the team in order that its members might work more effectively together.

As a part of reviewing the last meeting with the team, the coach had asked the team to initial where they thought they were in terms of the Adair model and the following is what resulted.

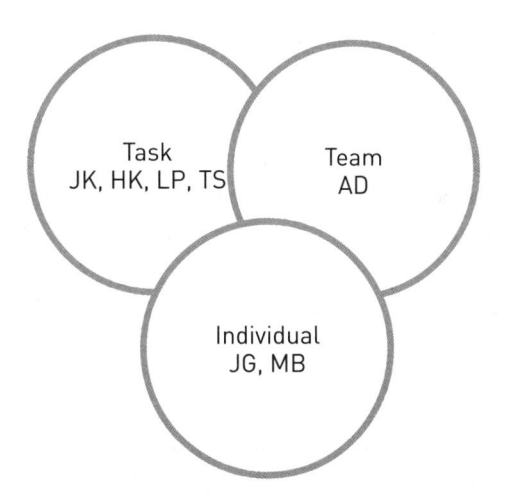

Task
JK, HK, LP, TS

Team
AD

Individual
JG, MB

### Coaching conversation

COACH: Thanks for doing that, what did it bring out for you?

JK: Well, I am totally focused on the task and I know we have a big time pressure here. I just want to get something down on paper. The head is going to expect results.

AD: I don't agree, Jim. I think if we just focus on the task we are going to miss a great opportunity.

COACH: Can you say more about that?

AD: I think that this is the first time we have met together as a team. Now, in order to make this curriculum work, we will need a great deal of co-operation between us. So, as a team, we are laying the foundations of what could be an exciting new way of working together cooperatively.

COACH: What do other people think of what Anne was saying there?

JG: Well, I find it difficult to work as a team when I am not clear at all about what we are supposed to be doing. I mean, I may be thick, but what actually is the task? How can we work together when we are not clear about what we are supposed to do?

JK: The task is to revise the curriculum to make it more competency based and personalised to the student.

JG: That's all very well, Jim, but, personally, I need something a bit more concrete than that to work on. I need it broken down a bit more. For instance, what is our task today, now?

MB: The other thing that I am not clear about is how we are going to work together. This is a mammoth task we have got here and there are all sorts of conflicting demands on this curriculum model. Are we all equals here? Is there a leader? What are we working towards? We have not even decided if we are going to take minutes. It strikes me that this is something new to all of us and before we go off to tackle the task we should get a few things sorted out.

COACH: So, what is it that you need to help you move forwards?

MB: I would like to establish some team protocols. For instance, have we got a team leader? What are our goals? What do we hope to achieve in each meeting? Also, what is your role?

COACH: My role?

MB: Yes, why are you here?

TS: I am sorry; look, I think that all this is a waste of time. We are all experienced professionals, we know how to run a meeting, for goodness sake. It is clear to me that we just need to focus on the end results. We can split the task up and do our bits and get on with it. We really have not got time for contemplating our navels with all that 'Why are we here?' stuff.

You can see from this discussion that the team was in the *Storming stage* at this point. There were team members who clearly had a need to define the purpose of the meeting before they could concentrate on the task. Other team members were very task-driven and wanted results. The only person who was fully team-orientated was AD who saw the opportunity that working together presented to this group.

The other thing that had happened was that the coach had not explained properly why he was there and needed to make that clear. As an external team coach, you really need to make your role clear. In this case, the head had asked the team coach to be present because he had employed him to work with the senior leadership team to great effect and now wanted to see more effective ways of working further down the school.

---

What this example shows is that people's learning styles mean that they will each need different things from the team. Some people will be happier focusing on the big picture without worrying about the detail. Others will not be able to focus on the end result until they have each stage worked out in detail. Some team members will want to know exactly the direction they are going in and what the steps are on the way, in a very linear way. Others will get bored with that and will want to try and focus on ideas.

The trick for the team is to use all the talents and skills of all the team members to best effect. In order for each team member to be in the area where the circles overlap – in other words the most effective working area – they will have to learn to tolerate and appreciate what others have to offer.

A team that has reached the performing stage will be able to accommodate the needs and styles of individuals and use its talents for the good of the team.

In the case of Wickfield School, the team did decide to work out what the roles and responsibilities were within the team. The coach asked each member of the team what it would take to make the team work more effectively and this is the list that they came up with.

1. To begin each meeting with a very short recap of what was agreed last time.
2. To start each meeting with what we hope to achieve by the end of that meeting.
3. To state common long-term goals.
4. To assign jobs to work on individually between meetings.
5. To build in time for reflection.
6. To allow an ideas storming session when a new task is set.

COACHING FOR SCHOOLS

They used this list to refer to at each meeting and, as a consequence, meetings became more productive. Review time was built into each team meeting, which was led by the team coach.

So, let us join the team again at one of its later meetings.

## Coaching conversation

JK: OK, so what you are saying is that the modern foreign language (MFL) department needs to do some fact-finding before we can go any further?

MB: Yes.

JK: So that is decided then, you will do that before the next meeting.

JG: There is just one thing that is worrying me here. I don't think that anyone has really given enough thought to the baccalaureate idea.

HK: Oh no, this is going backwards. I thought that we had ruled that out weeks ago.

JK: Hang on Harold, remember that Jane is an ideas person and we have used that well so far. Let's just have some time to think about what she has said. It may turn out to be a good idea. What do others think?

LP: I don't think it will suit the needs of the school at all. The employers are not ready for such a big change. They want better basic skills, not a whole new load of qualifications that they have not heard of.

JK: Jane what do you think? You have been very quiet.

JG: I can't just give an opinion on the baccalaureate just like that, I need some time to think about it.

COACH: Can we just have five minutes to review here? Can you use the Adair circles and tell me where you think you are.

JK: I feel that I am much more in the overlap zone. I understand the needs of individuals more, for instance, Jeremy is quieter and more effective but has a lot to offer. Jane may have held us up by throwing in the baccalaureate red herring but it may lead us down a really creative and interesting path who knows.

MB: It's all very well saying that but I still find it difficult. I just want to get the job done. Someone has to be like that or we would never get anything finished. I suppose I can see the value of debate more and that

> sometimes it is the process we are going through as a team that is making us more effective in the long run.
>
> JK: I really think that we are beginning to build on each other's strengths I would put us in the effective zone.

After the review, the coach asked the team members to put their initials in the parts of the Adair model that they thought they were in and this was the result.

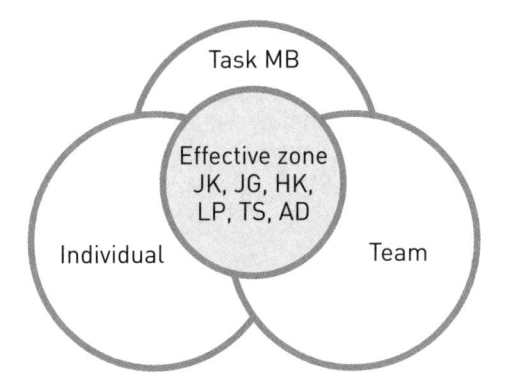

*Task MB*

*Effective zone*
*JK, JG, HK, LP, TS, AD*

*Individual*  *Team*

Clearly, with the help of the coach the team had moved forwards and was able to reach some of the characteristics of a learning team.

# The learning team

A school that has established a coaching culture throughout will want to have established 'learning teams'. There will already be a shared understanding of what coaching is and staff will be ready to use this approach in team meetings. A team may ask a member of another team to come to one of its meetings in order to review how it is operating. A team may be so practised in coaching that if may be able to do this for itself.

### What are the features of a learning team?

1. A team that regularly reviews the way it is working.
2. A team that has agreed goals and targets and reviews its own practice against them.
3. A team that balances the needs of the task, the team and the individual.

4. A team that has defined roles and responsibilities within it.
5. A team that will review the roles and responsibilities regularly.
6. A team that uses an external coach or has agreed to use coaching as a part of its agreed ways of working.

### Chapter summary

In this chapter we have used two models to look at the way that teams can work more effectively. Both have provided us with some features of the effective team. In addition to that, we have considered what a learning team looks like and how it operates. We have also examined how coaching the team can move it forward and have seen how a team coach can balance the needs of the team, the individual and the task.

## Your learning in practice

### Exercise

To put your learning into practice, consider one of the teams you are in and think about the following questions.

| |
|---|
| Rate the team out of ten against the features of a learning team. |
| What would it take to make this a ten? |
| What would you like the team to be doing? |
| What is getting in the way of this happening? |
| What does the team need to do to attain this? |
| Write an action plan with the team. |

# Coaching and distributed leadership

## This chapter in short

This chapter will be of interest to anyone in school who is in a leadership position. That includes subject leaders, SENCOs, members of the senior leadership team, deputy heads and headteachers.

The main theme of the chapter is to explain and explore what is meant by distributed leadership and to establish the relationship between coaching and this model of leadership. It will unpick the changing role of the school leader. It will find out who the school leaders are what they do and see how coaching can provide a framework within which they can lead. Through following a case study the chapter will unpick the relationship between coaching and delegating.

## Objectives

When you have completed this chapter you will be able to:

- explore the characteristics of the leader as coach;
- define the behaviours of the leader as coach;
- look at what distributed leadership requires of the leader;
- define the relationship between coaching and distributed leadership;
- provide a framework for developing delegation skills through coaching for the leader.

## Who are the school leaders?

School leadership is changing. It is becoming more distributed at all levels. Many different people in schools are now leaders with leadership responsibilities. The introduction of teaching and learning responsibilities (TLRs) marks a new emphasis on the leading of teaching and learning rather than on managing. It is intended to reward the leading of teaching and learning, placing less emphasis on the management of resources and pastoral areas. The responsibilities of a TLR allowance are to:

*Lead, manage and develop a subject or curriculum area; or to lead and manage pupil development across the curriculum area.*

TLRs also involve 'leading, developing and enhancing the teaching practice of other staff.' (DfES guidance – www.teachernet.gov.uk).

Any teacher in a school who is not newly qualified is expected to lead a subject area and will therefore be expected to lead the other staff in the development of that area.

Teaching assistants are also being given leadership responsibilities. As part of the remodelling agenda, there is now a set of standards for higher-level teaching assistants (HLTAs). One of those standards is to be 'able to guide where relevant the work of other adults supporting teaching and learning in the classroom'.

School bursars are also expected in many cases to lead a group of admin staff. The highly successful programme from the National College for School Leadership (NCSL), the Certificate of School Business Management, contains a unit on leadership. The programme is oversubscribed on every cohort. People in all spheres of school life have an expectation that they will receive professional development of a high quality. This professional development will need to include the skills involved in coaching. Coaching is an effective way of preparing staff for leadership roles and of building their leadership capacity while in the role. Very often people will assume a leadership role without any training. Coaching will provide that 'on the job' skills development needed for leadership.

This renewed emphasis on leadership will mean that staff need coaching from their leaders, who, in turn, will need to coach the staff in their teams. A subject leader, a member of the leadership team, a teacher with a TLR, an HLTA or school bursar with some leadership responsibility and the headteacher all will need to develop leadership skills and behaviours.

All these members of the school team will benefit from leadership coaching and should learn coaching skills so that they can develop their team and get them working effectively. For the rest of this chapter, the term 'leader' will mean a leader at all levels.

> **KEY POINT**
>
> In a school with a distributed leadership structure, more staff will be taking on a leadership role. Coaching can build up their leadership capacity to take on that role.

## Coaching and leadership styles

Everyone, at whatever level, will have their own style of leading. Hay/McBer has identified the six most common styles of leadership: coercive, authoritative, affiliate, democratic, pacesetting and coaching. Here is a summary of these leadership styles.

- **Coercive** – this type of leader will make demands on staff and expect immediate results.
- **Authorative** – this type of leader will present staff with a clearly defined vision. Leaders who demonstrate this style will be useful when morale is low.
- **Affiliative** – these leaders focus on relationships and view staff as friends rather than employees.
- **Democratic** – leaders in this category will rely on employee participation, which can lead to a lack of decision making.
- **Pacesetting** – these leaders will expect perfect and immediate performance from their staff. Their expectations are that staff will know what to do without being told.
- **Coaching** – leaders in this group will offer guidance to their staff and they will create a good climate in the staffroom (visit http://www.haygroup.co.uk).

We will all be able to recognise features of these leadership styles in the bosses we have worked with. Likewise we will be able to identify elements of some of the styles in our own leadership behaviours. If we are sharing out leadership in schools and making it more distributed, we will need to use a coaching style and develop the leadership capabilities of all staff.

> **Exercise**
>
> Think of yourself in your leadership role. Cast your mind back to the last time that you asked someone to carry something out. Which of the above styles did you use? How could you develop a coaching style?

## Distributed leadership and coaching

Distributed leadership is a way of sharing the decision-making process in schools. It is a way of dispersing the leadership responsibility throughout the school. A school with distributed leadership will have many leaders at different levels.

Distributed leadership in schools will mean a flatter leadership structure that is less hierarchical than before. Schools now have staffing structures that reflect the fact that more people in schools have a leadership responsibility. Leadership will become a function of everyone's job rather than the actual role. Leaders can take the opportunity to coach their staff on how to take on their leadership responsibilities.

As a result of this flatter management structure, there are fewer people at the top. School leaders are now expected to be multi-skilled and have good levels of emotional intelligence. Teambuilding and good communication skills are now requirements of not just the headteacher. Staff in schools are no longer satisfied with the traditional 'boss' telling them what to do. People at all levels in schools are keen to develop their own skills of managing and leading.

It is a fact that 40 per cent of school leaders will retire within the next five to ten years. With this in mind, the government has devised the 'fast track' scheme. The DfES' 'fast track' scheme aims to identify young teachers with leadership potential and help them achieve a senior leadership position within five years. It has spawned a group of young and ambitious people who want to make a career out of educational leadership and are keen to be given leadership experiences. In fact 'fast track' candidates are regularly advised on their leadership skills by their personal coach and given extra training.

There is a growing expectation among staff within a distributed leadership organisation that they will be coached by their line manager rather than being directed and controlled. Staff expect to be given opportunities to develop their skills and their leader can do this by coaching them.

## COACHING AND DISTRIBUTED LEADERSHIP

Some leaders will naturally have good interpersonal skills and their own leadership style will be a coaching one; others will have to learn those skills. The following is an example of a school leader using her learned coaching skills to move a member of staff forward.

This coaching conversation illustrates how someone new to leadership can be coached to grow into his/her role.

### Coaching conversation

Sue, a SENCO in a large secondary school, is coaching Deepa.

Deepa is an HLTA teaching assistant with responsibility for a team of four SEN teaching assistants. Deepa is new to this leadership role and is having monthly coaching sessions with Sue, who has been trained in coaching skills.

SUE: Now just remind me Deepa, what was the task we discussed last time that you had coming up?

DEEPA: I needed to organise the TAs to get all the resources needed for the end of year tests.

SUE: Yes, I remember, how did it go?

DEEPA: Badly, I ended up doing it all myself. I got so frustrated. I just don't think I am doing it right.

SUE: What actually happened?

DEEPA: I called them all together in a quick meeting during lunch and then I made it clear exactly what I wanted to happen. I made them a list and it said what had to go in each room, exactly as I stated. I made it clear what each individual child needed in the way of special requirements and I expected it done. The result was that only about half of the things were in place on time and the stuff that was there was not exactly how I had stipulated.

SUE: How did you feel about that?

DEEPA: Well, I felt really let down. I could not have made it any clearer; how can they have not understood? I felt very impatient, it took twice as long. I may as well have done it myself in the first place. I gained nothing by involving them at all.

| | |
|---|---|
| SUE: | Did you get any feedback from the TAs? |
| DEEPA: | Yes, they said that they did not know when the resources had to be in place by. The thing is that that is obvious; they should have been in place by the day before the assessments. Surely they don't need to be told that? |
| SUE: | What have you learned from this? |
| DEEPA: | Well, I suppose to be fair I could have given them a timeframe and made it clear when everything was to be done by. |
| SUE: | What about the way you speak to the TAs? You say that you make everything very clear and say exactly how things should be done. |
| DEEPA: | Yes, well obviously I needed to. Otherwise things may not be done in the way I want. |
| SUE: | The way you want? |
| DEEPA: | Yes, I have a way of doing it and I wanted them to do it that way. |
| SUE: | What did they think of that? |
| DEEPA: | I never asked them.... (Pause) Actually, I think that they may not have been that happy with it because Julie did have some suggestions but we did not have time to go into them. I probably could have started with asking them for their ideas. The only trouble with that is it would not have been done exactly the way I wanted. |
| SUE: | What would you have wanted instead? |
| DEEPA: | A combined effort I suppose. Working as a team. |

Sue went on to work with Deepa on forming a goal about adopting a less directive style with her team and getting them to work together collaboratively.

## How coaching helped

Through her coaching sessions Deepa began to realise that being a leader did not just constitute telling and directing people. She learned how to involve her team and delegate, giving them more ownership of the task.

# The leadership behaviours of a coaching style

We have already established that coaching is a skill that leaders in a distributed leadership organisation need to learn. Let's now explore what a coaching leader does and how they behave.

These are top ten leadership behaviours of a coaching leader.

1. Talk to your staff but listen more than talk.
2. Make your expectations of people clear so that they can succeed rather than fail.
3. Delegate clearly and effectively.
4. Be coached yourself.
5. Invite feedback on your own performance.
6. Build trust among your team.
7. Let go of the past and focus on the future.
8. If things go wrong do not ask why.
9. Demonstrate a high degree of emotional intelligence.
10. Be a helpful and supportive role model.

### Exercise

Look at this list carefully. How do you measure up? What is your weakest area and how would you work on it?

Having identified these ten leadership behaviours, let us examine in more detail what the indicators would be.

## Behaviour indicators

1. Talk to your staff but listen more than talk.
    - ☐ Taking time with staff and displaying those skills of listening to understand.
    - ☐ Not assuming that you know how your staff feel.
    - ☐ Building in time for coaching conversations.

2. Make your expectations of people clear so that they can succeed rather than fail.

    ☐ Making clear what success looks like in a given task.
    ☐ Assuming that people want to do a job well.

3. Delegate clearly and effectively.

    ☐ Using a structured system of delegation according to the needs of staff.
    ☐ Reviewing what your staff need to learn from the delegated tasks.

4. Be coached yourself.

    ☐ Reviewing your own goals regularly with a colleague or an executive coach.
    ☐ Working towards your own action plans.

5. Invite feedback on your own performance.

    ☐ Setting in place checks and measures that encourage all staff to give you feedback.
    ☐ Asking staff for informal and formal feedback in the form of questionnaires.

6. Build trust among your team.

    ☐ Taking personal responsibility for yourself.
    ☐ Treating people fairly and consistently.

7. Let go of the past and focus on the future.

    ☐ Encouraging a culture where continuous improvement and moving forward is the norm.
    ☐ When coaching staff do not encourage any dwelling on the past, instead focus on change.

8. If things go wrong do not ask why.

    ☐ Asking what happened and what can we learn from it.
    ☐ Making sure that more attention is focused on what went well rather than what did not.

9. Demonstrate a high degree of emotional intelligence.

    ☐ Learning to manage and recognise your own emotions.
    ☐ Being aware of the emotional climate of your school and the effect it has on others.

10. Be a helpful and supportive role model.
    - ☐ Be serious about your own professional development and focus on what you need to learn.
    - ☐ Keep the school's vision and values and the difference you are making to children at the heart of everything that you do.
    - ☐ Take risks and learn to handle success and disappointment with equanimity.

> **KEY POINT**
>
> **Coaching skills and behaviours can be learned and get better with practice.**

> **Exercise**
>
> Look at the behaviour indicators above. Use it as a tick list for your own self-assessment. Keep it out for two weeks and every time you feel you are displaying one of these indicators, tick it. At the end of two weeks have a look at the ones that are not ticked. Make a goal and action plan about those behaviour indicators that need working on.
>
> Alternatively, give it to some colleagues and ask them to tick it when they see the behaviours displayed.

## Coaching and delegating to build distributed leadership

The ability to delegate can be crucial to a leader and is one of the key elements in building the capacity of a team. Team leaders often struggle under massive workloads because they can't or won't delegate. When coaching leaders on work–life balance, one of the many issues to come up is delegating. There are many reasons given for not delegating. The most common ones are:

- 'The others already have so much work to do I feel guilty asking them.'
- 'Explaining how to do it would take so long that I may as well do it myself.'
- 'I will have to do too much chasing so I may as well not bother.'

- 'It is going to cause me as much stress in the end.'
- 'They won't do it the way I would have done.'

## Barriers to delegating

Let's deal with those reasons individually.

**'The others already have so much work to do I feel guilty asking them.'**

Everyone in a school has a lot to do and that will not change. People will always talk about how busy they are. As a leader you will have to put up with the guilt of asking someone to do something. Look upon it as giving them an opportunity to grow and develop their skills. In a school where leadership is properly distributed, it is important to delegate to everyone and not just to the people who will not moan about how much they are already doing.

**'Explaining how to do it would take so long that I may as well do it myself.'**

Yes, explaining will take longer at first and you will have to be patient. Explaining will build leadership capacity. You will have to explain something fully the first time and the time that takes should be regarded as an investment. You will not have to do it in as much detail the next time. Remember the old adage, 'If you do what you have always done you will get what you have always got'. If you never take the time to explain, then you will always be doing everything yourself and that is clearly unsustainable.

**'I will have to do too much chasing so I may as well not bother.'**

If you delegate properly using the model illustrated on page 235, you will not be doing any chasing. When someone delegates to you it is easy to fall into the trap of waiting to be chased as a trigger for actually doing the task. Some people will not actually do anything until they are chased; that is why you need to use a system of delegating.

**'It is going to cause me as much stress in the end.'**

What causes you stress is ultimately up to you. If you delegate clearly and effectively using the model detailed further on page 235, it should take the stress out of delegating. However, delegating does mean letting go and maybe that is what is causing the stress.

**'They won't do it the way I would have done.'**

No they won't and the sooner you realise that the better. They will do it differently. The person you have delegated to will bring his/her own personal style to the task. How could the person carry out the task in exactly the same way

COACHING AND DISTRIBUTED LEADERSHIP

you would have done? That would be an impossibility. The notion of whether they have done it in a better or worse way is not useful. If you delegate a task, you need to make sure it is understood what in the task can be adapted and what needs to remain.

In order to look at delegation more closely we need to examine our case study.

## Case study

School: St Marks, a large primary with 450 pupils on roll

Context: A semi-rural town with below-average achievement levels on assessment on entry. Attainment at Key Stage 2 is average when compared to similar schools but below the national average.

Background: The staff member 20 full- and part-time (some job-share) teaching staff and ten teaching assistants. There are also three admin staff and the entire full- and part-time staff number 35. The school has grown over recent years due to a large housing estate being built nearby. The school is popular because it is a church school and the only all-through primary in the town. The headteacher has successfully built the school up over the last five years and now has a senior leadership team for the first time. She is receiving coaching from an executive coach.

We are going to follow Carol, the headteacher, through her progress in delegating to her senior leadership team and show how she uses a coaching technique to do that.

This is Carol's first session with her coach.

## Coaching conversation

COACH: Carol, thanks for filling in the pre-session questionnaire, which has helped me build up a picture of how things are here. I know that you wanted the focus of our work together to be on building leadership capacity in your team. What is it that you want to achieve eventually?

CAROL: What I want is a situation where I am not rushing around chasing my team all the time. I have a leadership team that is not taking enough initiative. Its members are waiting for me to tell them everything so I may as well do it myself. The governors have decided they want a more collaborative leadership structure and I am landed with it as one of my performance management objectives and it is just not working. How can I delegate to a bunch of people who do not know what to do unless I tell them?

COACH: So you don't want to be chasing your leadership team for things it should have done. What do you want?

CAROL: Well, I don't want to be the only one who makes decisions.

COACH: Can you put that into positive language?

CAROL: To build up a team that takes the initiative.

COACH: Is that all?

CAROL: No, it is to build up a senior leadership team that acts proactively and takes the initiative.

COACH: So Carol, if I came back to visit you in a year's time and this goal had been achieved, what would you be telling me about? What would you be experiencing?

CAROL: Oh, that is hard. I can't think. I suppose I have spent so long thinking about what is not happening I find it difficult to imagine what an ideal situation would be.

COACH: Well let's think about that. A team that is taking the initiative and acting proactively – what will it be doing and how will it affect you?

CAROL: OK, I want the team members to fulfil their job descriptions, to be anticipating the annual cycle of events at the school, for instance SAT analyses, and to have put into place all that is needed without me asking. I want them to be respected by the other staff and leading their teams effectively so that their team members are being coached and developed.

COACH: That's good, now can we look at wording your goal again?

CAROL: Fine, what about, 'To strengthen the leadership capacity of the SLT so that it is acting proactively and taking the initiative'?

COACH: Good, we know where we are going, so let's first have a look at where we are now. What is happening at the moment with your leadership structure here?

# COACHING AND DISTRIBUTED LEADERSHIP

Carol then went on to explain that, due to the rapid expansion of the school and the recent rise in staff numbers, she was not used to having a leadership team to delegate to. She was used to doing everything connected with leadership in the school herself. When the school was smaller it was easier to do her job. She saw leading from the front with everyone else following as her job as a headteacher. She thought that leading everything went with the job description. It was only recently that she had found it impossible to perform all the leadership tasks for the school single-handedly. She had also noticed that she was beginning to lose staff with leadership potential. Carol suspected that she had to change her own style of leadership in order to adapt to a more collaborative leadership structure. Governors had detected this and gently suggested that working on building a more collaborative senior leadership team should be one of her own performance management objectives.

Through talking to the coach she identified that the members of the new team did not have clearly identified roles and responsibilities and had not received any leadership training. Working with the coach she put together the following action plan, which ties into both the school improvement plan and her own annual performance objectives.

### Action plan for Carol Sanfield, St Mark's Primary School

**Goal**   To strengthen the leadership capacity of the SLT so that it is acting proactively and taking the initiative.

#### Strategies

- Building performance management targets of the SLT around its leadership responsibilities.
- Half-termly coaching meetings with Carol for each SLT member in which the SLT members are expected to be proactive and look ahead in terms of what needs doing strategically.
- The headteacher adopting a structured approach to delegation.

#### Milestones – expectations after six months

- Performance management interview will have taken place with SLT, and PM objectives are set with reference to individual responsibilities.
- SLT will have clarified members' roles and responsibilities and head will have outlined expectations.
- Head will share with SLT that this is one of her own PM objectives.

- SLT meetings agenda's will reflect the half-termly coaching sessions. Team members will come to them outlining what their strategic role will be in the forthcoming term.
- Tasks will be delegated in a structured way.

### Success criteria
- SLT anticipating required actions and acting strategically.
- SLT highly regarded by staff and visible as leaders.
- Delegation is operating effectively.

### Link to school improvement plan
Links to goal 5 'The school will identify and nurture the characteristics of effective leaders and build the capacity for its own staff to lead at many levels'.

---

The next coaching session took place two weeks later.

## Coaching conversation

COACH: Carol you have put together the action plan. Is there anything that could get in the way of it happening?

CAROL: Well, I suppose time is always an issue, but this is fairly high priority at the moment. Unless I have a more proactive team taking the load off me then I am going to go under.

COACH: Are there any other barriers to it being successful?

CAROL: No, I don't think so... (Silence) Um, it is really up to them... the team members, they have to rise to the challenge.

COACH: It is up to them?

CAROL: Yes.

COACH: What part will you play?

CAROL: Well, I will be making the delegation clear. I will be giving the support but I will not be doing the tasks; it really is up to them.

COACH: What will you be doing differently?

CAROL: I will be delegating.

# COACHING AND DISTRIBUTED LEADERSHIP

COACH: What else?

CAROL: I don't know... suppose I do need to act differently. I need to change as well; it is not only about the SLT.

COACH: Can you tell me what that looks like?

CAROL: Actually, yes, it is about me as well. I need to give them space. I am going to need to learn a new lot of behaviours. Actually, no, that's not it; the coaching behaviours are in me, they just have not come to the fore lately because of the structure of the school and the demands of the job. I do need to make sure that I can enable staff. I need to adapt my leadership style to more of a coaching one.

The coach then went on to take Carol through the list of coaching behaviours and characteristics so that she could identify the ones that she had to work on.

**How coaching helped**

The coach helped Carol realise that the success of the objective did not entirely rest with her colleagues. The changes were going to require her to act in a different way. She would have to facilitate the development of her staff by behaving differently, learning new skills and resurrecting old ones. The coach agreed to see Carol in three months' time to check on her progress.

Let's now catch up with Carol in the next session with her coach.

## Coaching conversation

COACH: So Carol, can you tell me about the progress towards your goal?

CAROL: Yes, it's going well – we have completed all the actions on the action plan and I feel it has been really successful.

COACH: Can you tell me more about that?

CAROL: Well, we have been able to match more closely the SLT's PM objectives with its leadership role in relation to the school improvement plan. This has meant that team members have a much closer understanding of how their jobs relate to the development of the school. Actually it is more than that. It means that they now know that what they do matters, they have a stake in the strategic direction of the school. I think that previously they thought it was something I did on my own.

COACH: What has been the effect on you of that?

CAROL: The effect has been that I feel lighter, I feel as if I am working with a team for a change. There is still a long way to go – they are coming to me still for too much direction and I don't want it to be like that.

COACH: Can you describe that?

CAROL: Yes, the individual coaching sessions with each SLT member are going well. We have been able to go back to the school's vision and tie it in with their areas of responsibility. This has clarified the vision and values for them. They then are more able to get on with the actions in their action plan. The problem then comes with carrying out the actions. They are still not sure what they have to come back to me on.

COACH: Can you give me an example?

CAROL: Yes, Steve is maths subject leader. Part of his action plan was to do some observations of Key Stage 2. It was on his action plan and we agreed that it would be done. During his coaching session it emerged that he was still waiting for me to fix up the supply for it to take place. I was assuming that had already happened and he was going to share the results of the observations with me. I don't know what went wrong.

COACH: So did he know that he had the authority to book supply?

CAROL: Well, I just assumed . . . I suppose he had never done it before. You know, this is the problem with delegating. How do I figure out how much scaffolding to give them and how do I know what they will need from me?

COACH: Can we just put that to one side for a moment as I want to ask you another question? What about your development, moving towards more of a coaching style?

CAROL: I am trying to listen more, but I frequently feel the pressure of time. What has helped is the structured coaching sessions. That's when I can use those listening skills and I feel that is quality time with individual team members. I have not been brave enough to ask for any feedback yet but that is planned; I will do that next term. I thought I would ask the team three questions: 'What do I do well that you would like me to carry on doing? What do I do that you would like me to stop doing? What don't I do that you would like me to do?'

# COACHING AND DISTRIBUTED LEADERSHIP

The coach then went on to identify the next goal with Carol, which was to delegate more effectively.

**How coaching helped**

The coach helped Carol identify that delegating was the main problem. Carol did not know how much to assume with her team and how much she needed to clarify and scaffold the tasks that she delegated. The coach then went on to suggest a model of delegating that Carol could use.

The model that the coach suggested Carol worked with is the one devised by Tim Brighouse. He devised a nine-point scale of delegating, which you adapt according to the needs and experience of the person to whom you are delegating. His argument is that most of the problem with delegating comes when there is a lack of clarity over what the task delegated entails.

The list is as follows.

## Delegation

There are nine levels of delegation. Before delegating a job, make sure that both you and the other person understand which of the styles you are using. It can save you a lot of future grief.

1. 'Look into this problem. Give me all the facts. I will decide what to do.'
2. 'Let me know the alternatives available, with the pros and cons of each. I will decide what to select.'
3. 'Let me know the criteria for your recommendation, which alternatives you have identified and which one appears best to you, with any risk identified. I will make the decision.'
4. 'Recommend a course of action for my approval.'
5. 'Let me know what you intend to do. Delay action until I approve.'
6. 'Let me know what you intend to do. Do it unless I say not to.'
7. 'Take action. Let me know what you did. Let me know how it turns out.'
8. 'Take action. Communicate with me only if your action is unsuccessful.'
9. 'Take action. No further communication with me is necessary.'

Tim Brighouse
(http://www.dfes.gov.uk/londonchallenge/docs/LCdecember05html.html)

With the coach, Carol decided to use the list in a particular way with her SLT. Carol was open with the SLT and shared that this was one of her performance management objectives. She also explained that, as well as them becoming more proactive, she was also trying to learn to use more of a coaching style of leadership. Carol was careful to explain that she was not doing this because the team was doing something wrong. Instead, the team was needing to react to changes in the staffing structure and the growing demands of the school itself.

She decided to share with the team members the nine levels of delegation and asked them to identify which level they thought that they needed for each task. The ninelevels of delegation then became a focus for her coaching sessions with theSLT. When she began to use the list she found that, although the levels varied, it was very rare that 6, 7, 8 and 9 were being employed. Naturally, when being given a lot more responsibility, people were quite conservative at first about how much autonomy they could handle. If tasks that were delegated were more familiar, then team members felt they could have a freer rein. Coaching sessions with individual SLT members focused on how to move up the levels and how that would be monitored.

As an example, Carol was working with Jason, who was responsible for assessment in the school. Jason's task was to review the school's current assessment and tracking procedures, which at that point used several different systems and were unwieldy.

Jason chose the third level of delegation for this task as it was quite a major one involving resources and the whole staff:

'Let me know the criteria for your recommendation, which alternatives you have identified and which one appears best to you, with any risk identified. I will make the decision.'

Jason felt confident with this level of delegation; he knew exactly what was expected of him. Carol was delighted when Jason produced a written report on the alternatives for the assessment cycle, detailing both the risks and costs of the systems at the time agreed by them both. In his report he made his recommendations with reasons. Carol felt that she was involved in the decision-making stage, which was all that was needed. Jason had done all the research and had not bothered Carol until he produced his report.

Carol gave the SLT a questionnaire each term to monitor its progress and ask which level of delegation its members thought they were ready for. In her interim report to the governors – six months into the objective – this is what she identified as having happened:

'SLT feel that delegation is operating much more effectively in order to promote the school vision and to offer valuable professional development. As each member becomes more confident in his/her role the level of delegation is increased. Using the Brighouse list, members grade their progress and questionnaires have revealed the following:

- beginning of autumn term: average of 5 ('Let me know what you intend to do. Delay the action until I approve');
- beginning of spring term: average of 6/7 ('Let me know what you intend to do. Do it unless I say not to' and 'Take action. Let me know what you did. Let me know how it turns out');
- beginning of summer term: 6, 7, 8, 9 dependent on the nature of the task and stages of development of the person (8 'Take action, communicate with me only if your action is unsuccessful', 9 'Take action. No further communication with me is necessary').

It is clear that through this structured approach to delegation the team had moved closer to being the proactive group that Carol was hoping for. Carol was quick to point out that in times of stress some of the team did seem to revert back to having to be reminded of their task, but Carol found that she could then refer them back to what had been agreed as to how they would tackle it.

However, Carol did encounter some problems. For example, one member of the team, Claire, was responsible for English throughout the school. It had been acknowledged that there was a problem with guided reading and how it was being implemented. With the curriculum loosening up and becoming more creative, Claire felt that it was not being implemented as systematically as required and she felt that this was a factor in the slightly disappointing reading SAT results.

During her monthly coaching session with Carol, Claire had identified that she would like to be delegated to on this project at level 8 ('Take action. Communicate with me only if your action is unsuccessful').

Carol was not happy about this and felt that she would like to be more involved. Claire felt at odds with this as she was fairly experienced and thought that she would welcome the challenge. Carol and Claire settled on delegation level 6 ('Let me know what you intend to do. Do it unless I say not to').

As a result of this, Claire felt undermined. The project went well and during their coaching sessions Carol realised that she should have demonstrated the coaching behaviour 'Build trust in your team'. It was a lesson for Carol and it taught her that what Claire actually needed was not more support form Carol but to feel she could trust her own instinct about how much support she needed. It was about giving people what *they* think they need rather than what *we* think they need.

Let's return to Carol and her coach a year after she began work on her objective.

## Coaching conversation

COACH: So Carol, let us review the progress towards your goal. Tell me about what has happened.

CAROL: Yes, it has gone really well. I feel that the SLT is working independently and is stronger for it. Something else that has happened is other members of staff are valuing its members more highly and deferring to them rather than to me. They are much more highly regarded by the other staff.

COACH: How do you know?

CAROL: I used a questionnaire and one of the questions was about how effectively they thought that they were being led. I can just tell anyway, around the school people are not coming to me as much.

COACH: Can you give me an example?

CAROL: Well, there was an incident the other day about parents' evenings. One of the NQTs was a bit worried and did not know what to expect. Now in the old days she would have come to me and asked what to do. Her team leader had anticipated this and made some notes and went through it with her. Now, to me, that is an example of being proactive.

COACH: Yet, from the tone of your voice you don't seem too happy about it.

CAROL: Well, it made me think. I would have done that a while ago. I would have been the one to put things right and make it happen and now there are three other people who can do that just as well. I have wanted this for a long time and now I am having trouble with it.

COACH: What are you having trouble with?

CAROL: The fact that it used to be very clear what I did. I was the leader, I made the decisions. I was good at it. As we identified, it was not sustainable, but at least I knew where I was.

COACHING AND DISTRIBUTED LEADERSHIP

> COACH: So where are you now?
>
> CAROL: Well, I don't know, it has left me thinking. I am the headteacher if I don't lead everything, what do I do?
>
> COACH: So what is your key role now?
>
> CAROL: I need to pare it down to the thing that no one else does. I suppose I am leading the leaders. The thing is, there is now a gap and I don't know how to fill it. I have always moaned about not having time to think strategically. I now have the time but I don't know how to do it. I need to take a back seat from the day-to-day and figure out where we go now. The thing is, though, I need to learn how to do that.
>
> COACH: Shall we make that your next goal?

### How coaching helped

Now her team had developed and Carol was pleased with the progress and development of her team. What the coach helped her realise was the next set of changes that were now needed. The coach enabled her to move on and change the way she worked within this distributed leadership structure.

## Resistors to distributed leadership

Some leaders will, like Carol, be worried about giving up or sharing their leadership role. They may fear that they will lose their power base if they adopt a coaching style. Coaching is a more collaborative and democratic relationship than the traditional boss directing the team model of leadership. In a hierarchical leadership structure it is clear what everyone is required to do and people do not stray outside of their roles. Control is built in and accountability is transparent. If leaders have a resistance to letting go of this element of control, they may need individual coaching to overcome these personal barriers. Some leaders may feel also that they do not have the required skills to coach successfully.

> **KEY POINT**
>
> Coaching is a way of leading. It is not a separate set of activities that the leader does.

Carol's team development was successful because she was being coached on issues to do with adopting more of a coaching leadership style. The other reason for her success was that not only was she receiving coaching but also she had already been on a coaching skills course herself.

In Chapter 7 we saw how to introduce a coaching culture in to your school. A model of training staff in coaching skills was introduced. Let us take that one step further and look at how coaching can be used in a structured way to build a distributed network of leadership within the school.

### Step one

Train all staff in coaching skills using the model in Chapter 7.

### Step two

Establish a staffing structure that devolves leadership within the school. This will involve defining teams, identifying their leaders and sorting out what their roles and responsibilities are.

### Step three

Tie in the performance management leadership objectives with developing a coaching leadership style.

### Step four

Make sure whoever is leading the organisation is being coached.

### Step five

Set up regular coaching sessions for the senior team leaders. When that is well established, involve the middle leaders in coaching their teams.

### Step six

Monitor progress by encouraging questionnaires and regular feedback.

COACHING AND DISTRIBUTED LEADERSHIP

Team leaders can conduct coaching sessions using the LEAP model outlined in Chapter 3. The role of the team leader will be to make sure that the goals set in the sessions relate directly to the school's vision and values.

> **Chapter summary**
>
> This chapter has explored what is required of a leader in a school where there is distributed leadership. It has examined the part that coaching can play in building the leadership capacity of both the leader and the team. Finally, it has illustrated a way of structuring delegation in an organised way.

## Learning review

Who are the leaders in your school? Are you one of them and are you being coached on your leadership skills? As a leader or as coach, how will you have to adjust your behaviours? How could you practise some of the coaching behaviours in your daily work? Make a plan of how this is going to happen.

## Next steps

There are many different applications of coaching in schools. The more skilled and practised you become, the more you will bring coaching skills and the coaching framework into many of your school's daily tasks and interactions. Below are some of the ones that are most obvious.

### Coaching and 'Every Child Matters'

The five outcomes of 'Every Child Matters' mean that schools are being asked to look beyond the academic achievements of the child and work with outside agencies to develop the whole child. A coaching approach can be used with children to achieve the five outcomes of 'Every Child Matters'.

*Be healthy* – children can be encouraged to set goals and achieve them relating to a healthy lifestyle.

*Stay safe* – coaching can be used by lunchtime supervisors to encourage children to resolve playground conflicts and avoid being bullied.

*Enjoy and achieve* – children can be coached by learning mentors who can set goals relating to attendance and behaviour as well as academic achievement.

*Make a positive contribution* – a coaching approach can be used with the school's council encouraging children to make positive decisions to support the school community.

*Achieve economic well-being* – young people can be given careers coaching to ensure that they can achieve economic independence in later life.

## Coaching and parents

Many schools are already involved with the Basic Skills Council in running workshops for parents to improve their own literacy skills. Workshops in some children's centres now include parenting classes. A coaching approach can be used with parents who are struggling with their children's behaviour at home. Parents can be encouraged to set goals with their children and work through them, setting targets for good behaviour at home.

## Coaching and governors

Many governing bodies will have their own improvement plans or will be part of the school's SIP on the school's development plan. In Chapter 9 we looked at 'Coaching the team'. The governing body is a team. It needs to be coached into setting goals, making plans and working together effectively. Governors could start each academic year by trying to measure how effective they are and how they could improve by asking themselves a series of coaching questions. They should devote at least two sessions a year to coaching themselves on working as a team. Someone on the governing body could act as the coach or it could ask for a facilitator from the LA.

# Get going with being a coach

Previous chapters have dealt with coaching methods. We have looked at the skills involved in coaching. We have examined a model of how to do it. We have looked in some detail at ways in which coaching can be used in schools. In this last section of the book, the message is 'Just get on with it'. There is a coach inside of you just waiting to be released. You have the potential to be a coach. You just need to make a start.

You may be in the lucky position of already having received some training in coaching skills. You may be in a leadership position that enables you to introduce

# COACHING AND DISTRIBUTED LEADERSHIP

coaching through an INSET day. Alternatively, you may be reading this book with no formal training or time set aside for starting coaching at all. If that is the case – just do it.

## Put it into practice

You cannot become a skilled coach by reading about it; you need to take every opportunity you can to practise coaching.

Next time a colleague asks your advice, first ask him/her what he/she would do and what he/she has already done. Very often people have the answers and solutions to their problems within them. Think how much more satisfying for them it will be if you help them find their own answers.

In the staffroom, when people are talking, make sure that you are listening to understand rather than getting your next question ready in your head. When a parent comes in to complain about something, make sure that you really try to understand what he/she is saying. Try to form a picture of his/her reality of the situation as seen in his/her head before getting defensive and offering your side of the story.

When you are seeing a child because he/she has done something wrong, don't ask why he/she did it. Get him/her to tell you what happened and how he/she felt. Get him/her to tell you it was wrong.

You can practise coaching in formal and informal situations at home and at work. As a novice coach, you need to take every opportunity to use those listening, questioning and rapport-building skills.

## Co-coaching

One effective way to start coaching is to have a coaching partner, who could be a colleague or friend. You need to form an agreement that you will coach each other and practise your skills. You both need to find an issue to be coached on that is current and the outcome of which will make a real difference to you. It is important to realise that this is not role play. If the issues are not real then the coaching sessions will not work. If your co-coaching partner does not work or live near you then you could use the telephone to do your coaching sessions. Telephone coaching can be a very effective method of coaching; it is best with someone you already have a rapport with.

Co-coaching works best with three people. One person can be the coach, one can be the learner and one can offer observation and feedback to the coach. Three-way telephone coaching can be set up easily by using the conference call facility of the telephone. Coaching in threes also offers the added benefits of being exposed to three different styles of coaching. Co-coaching will also offer you the chance to develop your skills of giving and receiving feedback. If you are brave enough, recording your coaching sessions on video or audio tapes can be a powerful tool for learning about your behaviours as a coach.

When learning to be a coach, it is important to regard yourself as a learner. Setting yourself learning goals, making a plan and reviewing your progress are all ways in which you can achieve your best results.

## Use Internet resources

The following weblinks will provide more information about coaching and how to get started.

### *National Framework for Mentoring and Coaching*

**http://www.curee-paccts.com/dynamic/curee48.jsp#M&C**

The National Framework for Mentoring and Coaching is now available for viewing.

The new national framework for mentoring and coaching has been designed to provide practical and research-based support to practitioners and be a tool for making the work of the different agencies more coherent. It summarises why people do it, who gets involved, what they do – when and where. It clarifies, too, key skills and principles – succinctly. Just four sides of A4, it is rooted in evidence and geared to practitioners.

### *What is a learning conversation?*

**http://www.gtce.org.uk/cpd_home/learningconversation**

All teachers can think of a conversation that has changed their professional practice, but was it a happy accident or the result of a structured approach to professional learning?

A learning conversation is a planned and systematic approach to professional dialogue that supports teachers to reflect their practice. As a result, the teacher gains new knowledge and uses it to improve his/her teaching.

The General Teaching Council (GTC) spring 2004 survey of more than 4,000 teachers shows that a substantial majority gain their inspiration for their most effective lessons from talking with colleagues. The survey also reveals the extent to which teachers engage in and value learning conversations with their colleagues as part of their professional development. Almost all (97 per cent) say they have engaged in professional, knowledge-sharing conversations with their colleagues. For further findings visit the 2004 Teacher Survey page.

## COACHING AND DISTRIBUTED LEADERSHIP

### *Leading Coaching in Schools*

http://www.gtce.org.uk/networks/connect/connect8/c8ncslopportunities/c8leadingcoaching

The National College for School Leadership has produced *Leading Coaching in Schools* – a practical guide for school leaders about the implications of the new National Framework for Mentoring and Coaching.

More than 50 per cent of heads say that they now spend significantly more time coaching colleagues than they did previously.

Developing coaching helps leaders address many of the key issues facing schools today, such as:

- school improvement;
- reshaping the workforce;
- succession planning;
- personalisation;
- standards;
- accountability.

### *School Matters: Coaching in Schools*

http://www.teachers.tv/strandProgramme.do?strandId=6&transmissionProgrammeId=191796

A 30-minute programme on Teachers' TV, it looks at the roles of teacher, governor, headteacher/senior manager, NQT, teaching assistant, administrative and support staff and responsibility posts.

Following a number of different coaching situations in action, the programme opens on day one of a three-day training session, with trainer Mike Hughes introducing the principles of coaching.

### *One-to-One Leadership*

http://www.ncsl.org.uk/media/F7B/42/holmes-one-to-one-summary.pdf

This study draws on interviews with ten primary headteachers who have identified that they regularly use a coaching style of leadership and shows how many have made coaching work for their schools.

# Index

accountability 153, 159–62
action planning 73–5, 131–2, 158–9, 175, 203
Adair, John 211

barriers to success 95–7
Basic Skills Council 242
benefits of coaching 2–3
body language 28, 29–30, 35
Brighouse, Tim 235

Certificate in School Business Administration 220
challenge 5, 63
change
   adaptation to 6
   leading and managing 152, 167–71
   resistance to 96–7, 126–8, 168–70
   sustainable 190–1
Chartered Management Institute 2
classroom observation, and performance management objectives 132–3
coaching arrangements sheet 56–7
coaching culture 4, 5–6, 81–101
coaching model (LEAP model) 59–75, 85, 115, 126, 154
coaching triads 92–4
co-coaching 243–4
confidence building 104–12
confidentiality 56
consultant leader programme 2
consultants 14

decision making 153
definition of coaching 3–4

delegation 153, 162, 164–7, 227–39
   barriers to 228–9
   nine-point scale 235
distributed leadership 219–41

emotional intelligence (EI) 42
empathy 40–2
environmental problems 95
evaluation *see* reflection/evaluation
'Every Child Matters' agenda 196, 241–2
expectations, clarification of 12–14, 13–14

'fast track' leadership scheme 222
feedback, giving and receiving 133–8, 140–1
first session 57–9
flow, state of 111
frequency of sessions 55
future thinking 17–18

General Teaching Council (GTC) 244–5
goal setting 62–5, 66, 175, 177–81, 202
goals
   measurability of 63–4
   visioning 64–5
good practice, sharing of 3
governors 242

In-Service Education and Training (INSET) 19
individual coaching 7–8
interpretation 37–8
introducing coaching 82–3

judgement, suspension of 38–40

# INDEX

language *see* linguistic styles
leadership
    distributed 219–41
    'fast track' 222
    middle 146–72
leadership behaviours 225–7
leadership development 191–2
leadership styles 221
    leader as coach 99, 100
    leader as expert 98–9, 100
'Leading from the middle' programme 2, 150
LEAP model 59–75, 85, 115, 126, 154
learning conversation 244–5
learning styles 26–7, 143
learning teams 211, 217–18
linguistic styles 26–9
listening
    directed 32, 40
    surface 32
listening for learning 30–42
    empathy 40–2
    summarising and reflecting back 36–7
    suspending judgements 38–40
    switching off your inner dialogue 33–5
    using non-verbal signs 35
listening for meaning 91
location of sessions 55, 95

mentoring, similarities and differences 8–10
middle leadership 146–72
mistakes, learning from 5
model for coaching *see* coaching model
motivating staff 162–3
motivational triangle 163

National College for School Leadership
    (NCSL) 2, 150, 191, 220, 245
National Framework for Mentoring and
    Coaching 244, 245
non-verbal signals *see* body language
note-taking, responsibility for 56

parents 242
peer coaching 112–19
performance management 120–45
    monitoring stage 132–9

objectives 128–31
planning stage 122–31
purposes of 121–2
review stage 139–44
planning action 73–5, 131–2, 158–9, 175, 203
planning sessions 94
possibilities, analysis of 69–72, 203
potential, realisation of 103–4
practice sessions 92–4
praise 3, 140
pre-coaching meeting 54–5
Primary Strategy 2
professional development 5, 18–21, 143, 144
pupils, use with 6

questions 42–50
    challenging 45–7
    closed 44
    exploratory 48–9
    open 44–5
    powerful 49–50
    visionary 47–8

rapport building 25–30
reality, exploration of 66–8, 203
reflecting back 36
reflection/evaluation 5, 143
    and school improvement planning 176,
        182–90
resistance to change 96–7, 126–8, 168–70
respect 56
responsibility, acceptance of 15–17, 96

school bursars 220
school improvement cycle 176–7
school improvement planning 84, 174–93
scope of sessions 59
self-assessment 124, 139–40, 152–3
skills of coaching 24–52
Slatcher, Kate 5
sports coaching 4
staff development 5, 18–21, 143, 144
standards, evaluation of 153
strategic development 154–9, 173–93
summarising 36
sympathy 40

# INDEX

teaching assistants 220
teaching and learning
    responsibilities (TLRs) 220
team coaching 7, 8, 210–18
team development 204–10
teams 195–201
    balancing the needs of 210–17
    characteristics of effective 197–201
telephone coaching 243–4

time factors 55, 95–6
timings of sessions 55, 95
Training and Development Agency (TDA) 2, 121
Tuckman, Bruce 204

values 174–5, 176
vision 174–5, 176
    formation and articulation of 157–8